Garage

Life in the Offbeat Import Car Shop

Parker House Publishing Inc.
1826 Tower Drive
Stillwater, Minnesota 55082, USA
www.parkerhousepublishing.com

ISBN-13: 978-1-935350-03-3

Design: Paul Calver
Cover design: Paul Calver from a concept by Chris Fayers
Editor: Adam Swenson, Swike Creative

Manufactured in China through World Print Limited, Kowloon, Hong Kong

10 9 8 7 6 5 4 3 2 1

The **Art** and **Culture** of
California's Garages

Garage

Life in the Offbeat Import Car Shop

Simon Green

PARKER
HOUSE

Contents

Foreword

by Robert Goldman of
Moss Motors
Goleta, California

From the dawn of motoring until the end of World War II, the majority of Americans who could afford to buy a car had little choice but to buy something domestically made. Except of course if you happened to reside in Hollywood and were motivated to show off your European exotic.

After the war, car development and production capabilities accelerated—as they did, manufacturers from around the world started to dream of the biggest market in the world, and export sales into it.

Throughout the fifties, American cars became bigger, bolder, and more luxurious. A few European manufacturers found American buyers for their cars, though nothing that could be construed as serious competition to the homegrown product. The post WWII boom began shortly after the war ended with the American GI returning home with, more often than not, a small European two-seater. With American money in their pockets, who can blame a young GI having eyes for an MG or a Triumph, a Jaguar or an Austin-Healey, and wanting to bring it home? The postwar British government played their part, too, by strongly encouraging export sales in the face of a "controlled" war torn home market.

By the late 1960s and early 1970s the accumulated number of European cars imported into the United States, particularly from Great Britain, had grown into hundreds of thousands. The British sports car was, indeed, its own phenomenon. It introduced lightweight, spirited performance – both umph and handling – and a certain sense of freedom. Soon buying a British MG or an Italian Alfa Romeo or a German Porsche didn't seem so risky. Not that it was the only import car phenomenon. Following in those British footsteps, but starting a little later and without the help of many American Servicemen, was Volkswagen. And least we should forget, Hollywood and others who breathed the necessary rarified air had not stopped importing the likes of Rolls-Royce and Mercedes-Benz.

Here with the VW was a small car which would ultimately finish off the job started by the British sports car in turning America's automotive world upside down. While American whales were being sold on the "bigger is better" principle, the Bug - just like most of its British cousins - was an unapologetic minnow. Where domestic design was about chasing more horsepower, the Bug whistled along on less, and where the local products had been growing ever more luxurious, the only thing noticeably excessive about a Vee Dub was its frugality. Somehow, against all odds, the American people liked it— everywhere but in California.

Californians didn't like the little Bug: they loved it. Take a look at any movie with scenes set on Californian streets—from the fifties right through the seventies—and all you'll see are infinite quantities of VWs, along with the other Eurocentric imports, peppering the background.

The little Bug was so well priced that a new strata of society were finally able to afford a brand new car. Once they'd bought one, they weren't disappointed. Volkswagen had created a car that could carry four people in comfort and cruise all day on the highway, yet only use one tank of gas per decade—well, nearly.

The British sports car was, indeed, its own phenomenom.

Foreword

Added to that, the car almost never broke down, cost peanuts to service, and best of all retained incredible resale value due to the slowly-evolving design, and sales of all European cars continued to boom.

While this Euro car phenomenon spread across most of the U.S., California once again surged ahead. Think Japanese, of course, although these cars are not covered within. And a new term was created to embrace them all – the import.

Inevitably, as the years have rolled on, the older European models lost their edge, but the various models of replacement vehicles were good enough to keep customers loyal. Many of the original MG and VW owners are still driving import cars; they've just progressed to the modern breed of high-performance bolides.

As the cars have evolved, so have the workshops which exist to service them. From the one-man-band operations rebuilding just a handful of vintage Porsches every year to the vast service facilities which keep vehicles from a multitude of manufacturers, large and small, purring as smoothly as the day they left the factory, it's all in here.

Why California embraced these imported brands so much more readily than any other state is open to anyone's guess: the top-down driver's climate? The enormous variety of roads, resulting from its ever-changing terrain? The influence of Hollywood celebrities wanting to be seen in sporty, expensive, imported vehicles? The multicultural history of so many of its cities? Maybe it's a combination of all these reasons, and more. Nobody knows for sure, but one thing's certain—California's love affair with imported cars has created a diversity of automotive businesses unparalleled by any other American state.

If you love import cars too, maybe the why doesn't matter: the fact is that California remains the spiritual home of the European – the import - car in North America.

I hope you enjoy discovering some of its most skilled specialist workshops in this innovative book as much as I did.

As the cars have evolved,
so have the workshops
which exist to service them.

Autobahn

444 Vernon Way

El Cajon, California 92020

619-444-2290

All of the specialist workshops in this book exist to keep European cars going. Most of the shops do this by either rebuilding worn-out major components or replacing defective parts on their customer's vehicles.

The typical scenario is that a car would come limping in and leave running perfectly.

Autobahn is a business where most cars come in running fine but leave gradually in hundreds of pieces. That may not sound very constructive, but it most definitely is.

The business is owned by two young guys named John Whitelock and Sean Steele, and their shop exists to dismantle BMWs and Porsches, ultimately selling the parts worldwide.

The company has been in business for about twenty years, but Whitelock and Steele bought it around nine years ago. Both had been working in the automotive business (specifically with BMWs) so when they heard that Autobahn was for sale, buying it was quite a logical progression.

The typical scenario at Autobahn would be for them to buy an accident-damaged BMW or Porsche vehicle, then have their two employees tear it down piece by piece. The various component parts are then checked and organized into the relevant areas within Autobahn's cavernous building.

The typical scenario is that a car would come limping in and leave running perfectly.

Meanwhile John and Sean are handling the sales end of the business. Approximately one-third of the parts are sold to other workshops that are repairing a customer's vehicle, another third are sold via the Internet, and the remaining third are sold to local BMW and Porsche enthusiasts. While they specialize in the two brands, they find that BMW accounts for a much greater sales volume than Porsche. The reason is simple: there are more Bimmers on the road.

Autobahn

Autobahn dismantles vehicles from the sixties through to nearly-new cars, so their inventory effectively covers several eras of design. Apparently the "sweet spot" for their business is parts from around 1990 to the early 2000s, meaning any vehicles that are out of manufacturer's warranty. Obviously nobody is going to take a mid-nineties five-series BMW into a franchised dealership for a tune up, as the bill would probably exceed the value of the car, so the owners of these cars view Autobahn as a lifeline.

Dismantling these cars gives the owners of numerous pre-owned BMWs and Porsches a much cheaper way to buy parts. But the guys at Autobahn are proud that they're not only saving their customers a lot of money, they're also reducing the need to keep remanufacturing new replacement components. In California, most businesses give these issues serious consideration.

Along with recycling car parts, Sean and John also recycle any otherwise useless steel, aluminum, or copper parts that come off of the vehicles, plus the coolants and oils.

Some people are saddened to see cars being dismantled for parts, but John sums it up quite succinctly: "Some cars must die, so others can live."

Looking at the big picture, a relatively small amount of damaged BMWs and Porsches come into Autobahn to be dismantled for their valuable parts, but those parts ultimately head off in every direction of the compass to keep an enormous quantity of similar cars running the way they were designed to. It's a fair trade.

"Some cars must die, so others can live."

Barber's Shop Automotive

1116 18th Street

Sacramento, California 95814

916-448-6422

Car workshops are by their very nature quite spacious: they always rely on having enough space for the cars they work on. In current times, this typically locates the business outside of towns and cities, where land is less expensive.

There are, of course, exceptions to every rule. In Sacramento back in 1978, downtown land was reasonably affordable, and there was a local need for a workshop specializing in European cars. Operating downtown came with an added benefit: the customers could drop their car off for service, then walk to the office.

The shop in question was, and still is, called Barber's Shop. Though it sounds like you'd go there for a short back and sides, it's actually a car garage specializing in Alfa Romeos. Alfas are what they started with, and even though they added Ferraris, Lamborghinis, and Maseratis over the years, they've gradually drifted back to working mostly on the original Alfas.

Operating downtown came with an added benefit: the customers could drop their car off for service, then walk to the office.

When Barber's Shop first started, Alfa Romeos were current production cars, sold through franchised dealerships all across the U.S. Now Alfas are solely classic and vintage vehicles—at least as far as American owners are concerned. Yes, Alfa Romeo still makes great cars, but they haven't imported any into the U.S. for many years. To a shop specializing in Alfas, this means that all of their customer's cars are slowly aging and therefore leading quieter lives.

Barber's manager, Suntino Soldano, finds that most of the locally-owned Alfas are still used quite enthusiastically by their owners, but there's been a gradual shift from year-round use to fair-weather driving.

As springtime approaches, the cars all come in for a service or to fix those problems caused by inactivity. As the year rolls on, some owners start thinking about getting restoration work done over the wintertime.

Bucking the trend, Barber's still does all this work in their original downtown location, right in the heart of Sacramento. With the patina present in every part of the building caused by decades of hard work—plus the infinite amount of knick-knacks, classic signs, and vintage parts decorating the walls—it has become something of a legend in the region. Locals are always telling them, "Don't ever change. This is what makes this town cool."

The shop is unusual enough that it has even been used as a backdrop for photo shoots.

Barber's Shop Automotive

This request undoubtedly applies to the staff at Barber's as much as to the charismatic old building. Suntino lives for the cars and bikes which fill the workshop: he has his own early seventies Alfa GTV in daily use, plus a Moto Guzzi motorcycle and a collection of around ten vintage Vespas, another one of the shop's specialties. Comprehensive knowledge of scooters and classic Italian motorcycles isn't an ingredient of your typical car workshop, but this place is far from a typical workshop.

It's worth going in for a look at Barber's if you're in the area. If you do, don't worry: your visit won't come as a surprise. The staff are quite used to people having a look at the place—it's almost like a local museum. The shop is unusual enough that it has even been used as a backdrop for photo shoots. As eccentric as this all seems to most people, to the staff of Barber's it's just another day at work.

If you go for a nose around, remember to be respectful and let them get on with their work. After all, that is what's kept this place ticking away unchanged for the last thirty-some years.

Beckman Metalworks

Steve Beckman

644 Terminal Way

Costa Mesa, California 92627

949-574-2557

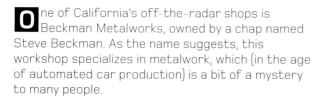

One of California's off-the-radar shops is Beckman Metalworks, owned by a chap named Steve Beckman. As the name suggests, this workshop specializes in metalwork, which (in the age of automated car production) is a bit of a mystery to many people.

Back in the days before car-building machines, real live people built car bodies. It still happens with some low-volume car production companies, but very few of those exist anymore. We live in an age dominated by mass production and corporations which makes what happens at Beckman's all the more impressive.

Steve and his employees build everything from obsolete pieces of metal trim to a complete car shell using nothing more than flat sheets of steel, brass, or alloy. Ideally their work will start with a complete vehicle that has been damaged by corrosion or some kind of accident. Sometimes all they're given is a rolling chassis and some old photographs.

In the case of an existing car, they will either use templates or digitize the body. They'll then painstakingly recreate a new shell from those reference points. When all they're given is a photograph, things are much harder. They have to calculate body dimensions from known measurements, such as the diameter of a wheel rim. With a project like this, the more photographs, the better. To mere mortals it's daunting stuff. To Steve it's just simple reverse engineering.

One of the employees at Beckman's is a 78-years-young fellow who's been a metal man his whole life: he's also the chap who initially taught Steve how to use the body man's favorite tool, the English wheel. This veteran now works half days and concentrates on smaller, more intricate jobs— not everyone needs them to create a full body shell, after all.

In total, there are four very skilled workers in Beckman's body shop. The normal pattern (if there is such a thing) would see them working on four different projects. Sometimes if they're nearing completion on something, they'll all work on finishing the same vehicle. There are also three other guys working in his paint shop where they're always working on one car at a time.

The cars that roll through his doors vary wildly, but Ferraris are his chosen specialty. To Steve it's very satisfying to recreate an irreplaceable body from an era long gone. These cars can spend over a year and a half at the shop in extreme cases. These tend to be the cars that have a potentially high resale value—otherwise the owners simply couldn't justify such an incredible amount of work.

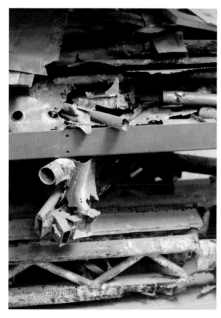

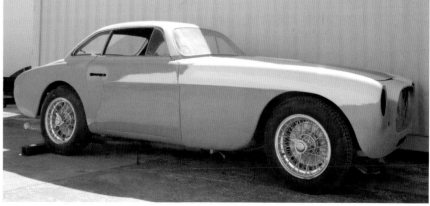

Back in the days before car-building machines, real live people built car bodies.

Without old-world craftsmen like Steve Beckman and his employees, many irreplaceable old cars would have simply been broken for parts. In some cases these cars are brought back from the brink of death, a point not lost on the few people allowed onto his very private premises.

Just how he works his magic will probably remain a mystery to most of us. Though he's never likely to give guided tours of his workshop, most of us have already seen the results of his handiwork at some prestigious car event—we just never knew it.

In total, there are four very skilled workers in Beckman's body shop.

Brian D. Moore Restorations

Brian D. Moore

2347 Gold River, Suite N

Gold River, California 95670

916-635-3559

Many of the workshops in California shy away from the bodywork side of the business. In the majority of cases, a place is either a mechanical shop or a body shop, but seldom both.

Nestled in a town on the Gold River in northern California is a highly-regarded body shop, Brian D. Moore Restorations, named after its founder and owner. There will be no medals awarded for those who figure out that the majority of Brian's work is in the full restoration of vehicles. He estimates that full restos account for eighty percent of his shop's work. The remainder comes from repair work—namely accident damage.

What isn't so obvious from his company's name is the type of vehicles he favors: high-end European cars, both current and classic.

His automotive obsession started when he was a kid. After he got out of high school he started working on private airplanes owned by people who "made a lot of money." When he got tired of that job, he drifted into working on "their toys." In the case of these people, "toys" translates into Maseratis, Lamborghinis, and Aston Martins.

This change happened back in 1978, so it's safe to assume that by this point in time Brian is unlikely to get tired of what he's now doing. Apparently the typical job would be for a customer to bring in a classic European car like the Porsche 911 shown in the accompanying photos. Brian will take the car apart and have it media blasted to take care of any rust. Then he'll do the metalwork and bodywork, and finally paint the car.

Whether he will reassemble the car depends on the customer: in the case of the orange 911, the car's owner wants to put it back together himself. Surprisingly a lot of his business comes from members of the public, not from other shops, though there are three mechanical specialists within his region that he does regularly work with.

In the photos you can also see a Corvette that Brian was restoring. This car differs from the Porsche, firstly in that the customer wants it to be completely finished by Brian before handover, and secondly in that it's not European made. This isn't really by choice!

In the majority of cases, a place is either a mechanical shop or a body shop, but seldom both.

Brian finds that most of his customers have collections of cars, and when he's restored one of their European cars, he'll often be asked to restore something else. In the case of the Vette it was a little less welcome, due to the fiberglass body. But Brian loves his customers, and really what small business owner would ever say no?

So, while Brian Moore is a European car restoration specialist, other cars come and go too. Some take six months, while others have been known to linger on for a couple of years. Brian works solo, after all. His son will help on a part-time basis, but at the core this is a "labor of love" for one man.

Yes, love is the most applicable term once more: Brian really does love these cars. He'll often find a Maserati, or something similar in Europe, and buy it for himself. He'll then take his time, restoring the car back to "as new" condition between other jobs. After enjoying it, he usually sells it because he's stumbled across another beautiful oldie, something different that he's always dreamed of owning.

His preference is apparently Italian cars from the fifties and early sixties, so there are still some rare cars out there that he lusts after.

Though most shops shy away from bodywork, as far as Brian Moore is concerned, it sure beats working on airplanes.

Yes, love is the most applicable term once more . . .

British Auto Specialists/Doctor Jaguar

Colby Calkin

1974 Placentia Avenue

Costa Mesa, California 92627

949-646-8802

This Costa Mesa establishment is a combination of two well-established, yet previously separate, British car shops. Doctor Jaguar had been in existence for twenty-eight years, and British Auto had been around for fourteen.

The original owner of British Auto decided to splinter off and concentrate on just the original Austin/Morris/BL "Mini" cars, and the original owner of Doctor Jag sold his business to the current owners but ended up staying on as an employee. Now both names operate under the same roof, and the 15,000 strong customer base from both shops is as loyal as ever. This makes for one busy workshop.

Jaguars are obviously one brand of car that you'd expect to see in the workshops, but British Auto is also known for Range Rovers and Land Rovers. Even Aston Martins regularly find their way in. Aside from their preferred brands, almost every other kind of British car will end up in the workshop at some point. When an owner trusts their Jaguar to a shop like this, it's predictable that they'll want them to work their magic on their MG or Triumph too.

Even within these brands, there's some real diversity to the vehicles that turn up at the shop: from the gorgeous 1928 Rolls-Royce Phantom to new Range Rovers, they see (and fix) it all.

Studying the accompanying photographs has probably already caused some heart palpitations: the pictured Jaguar D-type is actually a Lynx, which is driven almost daily.

. . . there's no real reason here to stop driving the classics.

For the uninitiated, the Lynx is a handmade replica of an original D-type, built around a donor E-type. This means that the end vehicle has much improved suspension over an original D-type, as the XKE was a later, more sophisticated, Jaguar design. The Lynx also has a much improved power output—about 300 horsepower.

The owner of this particular Lynx also had an Aston Martin DB6 in for a bit of tuning and tweaking at the time of our photo shoot. Unbelievably he drives this car regularly too, though apparently that's actually quite common here.

Colby Calkin, the young man organizing what goes on at British Auto, finds that because of the California climate his customers are likely to pick their Range Rover to drive to work on a Monday and their E-type on a Tuesday. It means that all of their customers' cars, ancient and modern, are regularly coming in and out of their workshops.

Doctor Jaguar had been in existence for twenty-eight years, and British Auto had been around for fourteen.

Of course, everything about using one of these classic beauties on a daily basis helps to further the old car scene. As old parts wear out, companies happily build and sell new ones. Specialist workshops develop a niche market fixing the cars, and the vehicles are never truly made obsolete.

If we stopped driving them, the parts sales (and potentially even their manufacture) could dry up completely. Then before you know it, a simple problem like a worn-out distributor could seriously endanger the life of your beloved old car.

Even in the rare case that a car is deemed beyond saving, either through accident damage or excessive rust, they can be remade into "new old cars" like the Lynx D-type. Considering that terminal corrosion is highly unlikely to happen in California—with their even, temperate climate postponing rust almost indefinitely—there's no real reason here to stop driving the classics.

So as long as there are shops like British Auto Specialists around, those Californians will be able to just keep racking up the miles.

British Car Service

Dan Kelly

2541 Tower Avenue, Suite D

Sacramento, California 95825

916-489-5361

The love of British cars certainly isn't exclusive to the residents of southern California: in the northern parts of the state there are just as many passionate Brit car owners. The Sacramento area is one of several spots with many such enthusiasts, and, when the time comes for their cars to go in for service or repair, it's time to find the right workshop.

If your British car is a newer model, still under factory warranty, then your choices are usually limited to the franchised dealerships, but (as with many other European built cars) most owners stop using the dealership once the car is out of factory warranty. Why so many customers jump ship and leave the franchised dealership as soon as they can is a complex enough issue to warrant a book of its own, so for now we're sticking to the choice of workshops available to those people who are free to choose.

The most well-known and seemingly popular British car specialist in this particular area is a shop called British Car Service, headed by a gentleman by the name of Dan Kelly. As soon as you walk through the doors of this shop, it's easy to see why British car enthusiasts instantly feel so at home here. The cars fill every inch of the workshop space, and the diversity of vehicles is staggering: there are Bentleys from 1937 to 2003, Austin-Healeys, Sunbeams, Land Rovers new and old, and many, many others. Owning a British car is a passion, and walking into this place is guaranteed to stir that emotion in anybody.

Dan has been running this business for nearly forty years, so he's obviously doing things the right way. Most of the work is repeat customers, and most of his new business comes from recommendation, which says everything you need to know.

. . . in the northern parts of the state there are just as many passionate Brit car owners.

They'll do pretty well everything at British Car Service—from basic maintenance to restoration—though they'll utilize a local body shop and upholsterer to help with restorations, as so many other shops do. One reason for this is that it's a totally different skill set. Another is that California has a very strict bunch of rules for any business within the automotive world, and most mechanical shops simply don't want to get involved with another set of complicated requirements.

He's found that his impressive personal collection adds credibility for those just meeting him.

As for the vehicles Dan and his team will work on, that varies as much as the cars visible in the photos. From 1940s to late model, they're equipped to deal with it all.

In the case of late model cars it means they have all of the software and diagnostic equipment necessary to work on anything out of warranty. Diagnostic equipment for modern cars is extremely expensive, so privately-owned businesses won't invest in equipment they can't use, which is why they're not usually set up for vehicles still within factory warranty.

Dan is still as passionate about British cars as the owners that seek him out. He personally owns a Jag XK120, two E-types, a Bentley Continental, '37, '51, and '62 Rolls–Royces, and a Series 3 Land Rover. He's found that his impressive personal collection adds credibility for those just meeting him.

If a customer has an old car which has sat unused in a garage for several years, seeing all of the other oldies in Dan's workshop makes them feel comfortable in letting him recommission their old car. Ultimately this means another old car gets brought to Dan's workshop, and thus the cycle continues . . .

British Heritage Motorsports

Randall Zoller

1437 Pioneer Way

El Cajon, California 92020

619-447-0025

trihard2@juno.com

The Triumph name is a magical one to car enthusiasts and motorcyclists the world over. Initially formed at the tail end of the nineteenth century, the Triumph company was established not to build motorcycles or cars, but bicycles. It's just as surprising to many people that such an immediately recognizable English brand was founded by two Germans.

By the start of the twentieth century they were also making motorcycles, and by the 1920s they'd purchased a car brand, which ultimately became the legend known simply as Triumph. The famed Donald Healey was employed as the company's GM— he would later be the man behind Austin-Healey, some Jensen models, and the Jensen-Healey sports cars.

Years down the line, the struggling motorcycle division of the Triumph Company was bought out by one business and the flagging car brand by another. However, by the fifties, both varieties of motorized Triumph were achieving incredible sales success in the U.S. By the late sixties, not only did most Triumph production end up going stateside, but also most development work was done to keep the enthusiastic American buyers happy.

In their heyday, a huge number of all types of Triumphs went to California, a place where people really appreciated such lightweight and nimble sports cars. The cars were fantastic on the racetrack, and so a bunch of Triumph tuning experts evolved, people like Randall Zoller of British Heritage Motorsports.

British Heritage Motorsports is based in El Cajon, east of San Diego. They're a workshop specializing in British cars in general, but Triumphs and Austin-Healeys specifically.

Over the years, Randy Zoller has restored just about every muscle car ever made, and quite a few exotic Italian cars too. He even built the motors for the California Spider cars featured in the famous old movie, *Ferris Bueller's Day Off*. With this kind of résumé, the respect he has for the Triumphs and Healeys says a lot about the quality of the brands.

At Heritage, Randy does everything from basic service and maintenance to full restorations. He finally stopped doing the body and paintwork himself once he found a local place skilled enough to achieve the results he expects. Spending less time doing body-related work means more time available for mechanical improvements—including tuning.

British Heritage Motorsports is one of very few places able to offer high-performance engineering improvements to these British sports cars. Randy even runs a racecar that showcases his shop's work, a very potent Triumph TR4. This race Triumph features a lengthy list of improvements, including a unique brake system featuring a twin master cylinder with a cockpit-mounted adjustable-bias system for front and rear brakes.

It also features an adjustable front sway bar, race springs, a coil-over-shock conversion for the solid rear end, and much more.

The car does very well in vintage racing, sometimes with Randy at the wheel. So when Heritage explains that they offer mild performance upgrades through to full race cars, you know they're not bragging.

Places like Heritage Motorsports used to be more common, but as the surviving cars get older, these specialist shops have become increasingly rare. The same was once true for the Triumph motorcycle brand, but since they were re-launched in the early nineties, the industry built around them has been completely rejuvenated.

Now all we need is for the current owners of the Triumph brand to realize the car still has many diehard fans and follow their lead.

Over the years, Randy Zoller has restored just about every muscle car ever made . . .

Bugformance

1620 El Camino Avenue

Sacramento, California 95815

916-929-4320

Southern California is well-known for its love of air-cooled Volkswagens, which is appropriate enough as huge numbers of these old vehicles were originally sold down there. SoCal is even home to some of the biggest VW gatherings, though many of these events are actually organized by a company out of Northern California.

Bugorama Promotions is located in Sacramento and runs several VW-themed enthusiast events around the country. The company is run by three brothers from the Hole family, and they are (as you might expect) Volkswagen nuts. What many people don't necessarily know is that the Hole family also owns and operates a large VW workshop, known as Bugformance.

Bugformance is quite possibly the focal point of Northern California's entire air-cooled VW scene, and their involvement in the scene runs very deep. Step into their showroom in Sacramento and you're greeted by friendly staff, which is no doubt due to the fact that it's one hundred percent family run. You're also greeted by a couple of thousand square feet of racks and walls covered in parts for early Vee Dubs. An impressive sight, but it's just the beginning.

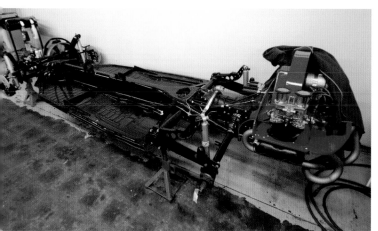

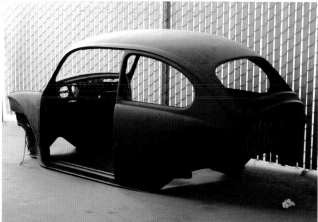

Head into the next room and they have an immaculately-restored floor pan (rolling chassis in VW lingo) from a '67 Bug, parked behind a fully-restored '67 Bug convertible. Both effectively showcase the quality of work undertaken in the workshops here. Behind the vast parts showroom are their workshops, which are even more expansive. Inside these shops they'll handle anything that an owner of a classic VW could ever ask for, from full restoration through to high performance engine builds.

Though Bugformance works on all VWs (they have fully up-to-date diagnostic equipment), they find that the majority of their work is the classic air-cooled models. As California has such strict smog laws, they can't even improve the performance of the new turbo motors, which are sent out of the factory in a relatively modest state of tune. Where other states can chip these modern vehicles, California can't.

SoCal is even home to some of the biggest VW gatherings . . .

Californian law also throws some obstacles in the way of their restoration work. Body shops are now almost solely run by body-only specialists—Bugformance sees good shops disappearing regularly since meeting the various requirements is so tricky. As a result they don't attempt to operate an in-house body and paint shop. That's the only work they send out.

Performance work, however, is done solely in-house, and it's something of a specialty here. Any fan of the early Volkswagens will know that the best factory motor ever created, still struggled to produce sixty horsepower. Bugformance has put together a motor package built around brand-new crankcases, bored out to 1915 cc, with improved cylinder heads and big carburetors. Their motor effortlessly puts out a much more respectable one hundred horsepower. They're so well know for these smog-legal motors that they build (from scratch) an average of three per week. During busy times they can even perfectly assemble two in a single day.

. . . they find that the majority of their work is the classic air-cooled models.

These motors are a huge hit with their customers, many of whom buy them as a unit to install themselves. Since engines like this, and all of the other parts required to keep these cars on the road, are so readily available, Bugs are still in common day-to-day usage in northern California.

Mike Hole says that a common in-house conversation topic concerns the ratio of daily drivers versus weekend cars within their customer base. They unanimously agree it's about half and half.

This must be one of the highest ratios seen within the classic car scene. Thirty years after the last air-cooled VWs landed in America, they've still got what many Californians look for in a car. As long as shops like Bugformance are around keeping them in tip-top shape, there's no reason that should ever change.

BW Auto Dismantlers

Jeff Buchanan

2031 P.F.E. Road

Roseville, California 95747

916-969-1600

In the northern California town of Roseville lies the region's biggest VW/Audi dismantling yard. Knowing that it's the biggest of its kind means that it's an exciting place to visit—if you're into VWs.

A visit to the yard is also a lesson in the changing face of auto dismantling. When it first opened in 1977, their core business was in the various models of air-cooled Volkswagens: the Bugs, Things, Buses, and Karmann Ghias. By the nineties, the cars being made at VW had changed dramatically, so the wrecking yards based around them changed too.

Now, most professionally-run wrecking yards loosely operate on a ten year rule. That means they'll prioritize the cars just out of warranty, going back for ten years. That's not to say it's all they'll stock, but, as it accounts for the majority of what people buy, it explains why they're the vehicles that most yards want to dismantle.

That phrase "yards want to dismantle" is very relevant. In the early days of almost every wrecking yard in the world, the customer would be sent by the grizzled owner into a vast field filled with precariously-balanced towers of cars to locate whatever it was they needed. Not any more.

A visit to the yard is also a lesson in the changing face of auto dismantling.

When Jeff Buchanan started running the business established by his father, he quickly stopped that practice. While it was common for people to remove their own parts in the old days, it was also common for them to damage a massive amount of other parts in the process. Jeff remembers how common it was for a kid to go back into their field and remove the small chrome escutcheon from the dashboard of a classic Bug, a part worth small change. Later they'd find he'd ruined the whole dash in the process. Now, if you want a part, an employee of the yard removes it for you.

Another major change came with the introduction of computerized inventory. Previously, a wrecking yard's owner would buy their vehicles based on a gut feeling. Now, the computer tells you exactly what you have, how long you've had it, plus what you've sold and when. This way owners recognize the slow-moving parts and the faster-moving ones, meaning that whole vehicles are bought only as required.

This is where an exception to the ten year rule comes in. Jeff has some slightly less typical vehicles in, like an '85 Vanagon and a Corrado. That's because if somebody does own one of these less common vehicles, they're usually really happy to finally find a yard that can sell them parts.

As you can tell, wrecking yards are more of an accurate science these days. When a vehicle has yielded most of its useful parts, the chassis is sold for scrap metal and replaced with another, a cycle that continues in perpetuity.

BW Auto Dismantlers

Scrap metal values reached an all time high in the fall of 2008, spurring Jeff into selling a huge amount of cars for their scrap value. Making decisions like this keeps the business running in an age where keeping your wits about you is essential.

As unbelievable as it may seem, even the auto dismantling industry is under threat from the irrepressible growth of the corporation. There are a couple of big firms currently buying up small yards to add to their empire, giving them the same buying power as the big boys within any industry. Where Jeff's yard may break a few hundred VWs a year, the big boys are now turning over 25,000 to 35,000 vehicles.

As intimidating as that must be to the owner of any smaller company, history continually shows us that big companies continue to move slower and fall harder. So for now, BW Auto Dismantlers is still the region's largest German car specialist—let's hope that it stays that way.

Another major change came
with the introduction of
computerized inventory.

Carrera Sport

Steve Bergen

(Somewhere north of) San Diego, California

In California there are a staggering amount of workshops, with varying degrees of relevance to European cars. Some places work on cars fresh out of the factory, and some work on cars so old that their factories have long since forgotten they even made them. The great majority of automotive workshops concentrate on the stuff right in the middle.

You can then further divide the shops: by the number of makes they'll work on, the depth of the work that they're willing to undertake, and finally the size of the operation. Specialized one-man-bands seem to be the rarest of the breed.

Steve Bergen runs a great little one-man-workshop called Carrera Sport, just north of San Diego. His chosen specialty also happens to be his true love, vintage Porsches. The origin of his passion for vintage Porsches is easy to trace: he helped his dad work on them when he was a kid. In fact, that's understating it somewhat: he once helped his father restore a beautiful '54 pre-A 356 coupe, a car that now resides at the Porsche museum in Stuttgart. That should say volumes about the quality of the work he was taught.

Now Steve is an avid early Porsche collector and also works on cars for a very select group of people. These are all folks who'd previously seen the quality of work that Steve puts into his own cars, and ultimately persuaded him to work on their cars too. Without the persuasion, there would be no business: Steve still has no interest in advertising or in rushing the work he agrees to.

That's not to say Steve is a slow worker, just that he's a perfectionist who works alone. Steve will happily show you around one of his own cars and point out what is "orig." Originality is king in the eyes of any true perfectionist, and Steve is no exception.

He'll point out the spare wheel on one of his own extremely well-preserved examples. He explains that the factory would use whatever paint they had in excess when priming wheels, then shoot it over with silver paint.

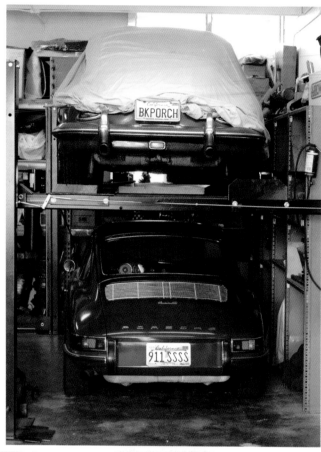

Specialized one-man-bands seem to be the rarest of the breed.

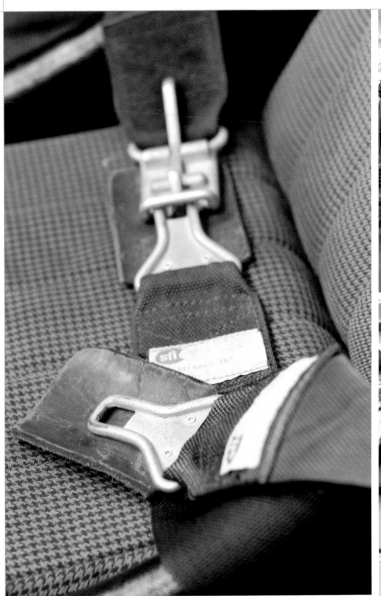

He'll point out what makes the car's high-tension cables distinguishable as the ones originally fitted by the Porsche factory, and explain how you can tell if the seats are still original or reupholstered. Learning every nook and cranny of these cars has never been a chore to Steve, but instead a wonderful exploration that has taken most of his life.

Originality is king in the eyes of any true perfectionist . . .

This isn't to say that every car he comes across is one hundred percent the way it left the Stuttgart factory, just that his greatest love is finding one of those rarest-of-the-rare unmolested survivors. When he comes across a car which has already seen a few modifications, a few improvements, he'll happily take them further down that route.

Take the "sunroof transplant," for example. Steve will locate a wrecked or rust-riddled early car with a factory-fitted sunroof. He'll carefully drill out the factory spot welds and over the course of a week or two, he'll fit it to a car with a standard roof. His work is so good that most "experts" wouldn't even know he'd done it.

Small shops like Steve's are the lifeblood of California's European car workshop scene. The biggest problem for the averge person is finding them, as shop owners like Steve really don't want to advertise!

Cavallo Motorsports

Scott D. Beyer

6010 Avenida Encinas

Carlsbad, California 92011

760-603-8321

Scott@cavallomotorsports.com

Sandwiched neatly between Los Angeles and San Diego is the town of Carlsbad. As the two major cities are not far from each other, a smaller, quieter location like this one can be perfect for the right business as it has the potential to pull in customers from both of the big neighboring metropolitan areas. Cavallo Motorsports, a workshop specializing in exotic European cars, is one such business.

Cavallo moved to their current location about a year ago after some changes in leadership led to growth, creating a need for bigger premises. The business itself is well established, having been around in its original form for many years before the recent upgrades.

The business is involved with most aspects of the European exotic car scene. They sell cars, both on consignment and their own vehicles. They also help customers with car acquisitions, sourcing anything from late-model vehicles right through to vintage race cars. Finally they'll undertake any work these vehicles may need, from basic maintenance right through to full-blown restorations.

Cavallo restorations are of the highest quality, often being completed for customers who intend to show the finished vehicle at Pebble Beach. That famous show is big business in this area, especially for a shop specializing in exotic European cars, as the quantities of these cars entered into the show is huge.

While the people who work at Cavallo Motorsports take immense pride in finishing their customers' cars to the better-than-new standards typically seen at Pebble Beach, they're even more passionate about another segment of their client base: racers. The shop (and its customers) are very active in the race scene, particularly the Ferrari North America Shell series.

Cavallo restorations are of the highest quality . . .

Cavallo Motorsports

The accompanying photographs show a diversity of vehicles quite typical in their workshops, though it's the brace of Jaguar D-types hidden under canvas covers that most effectively sum up the two diametrically-opposed directions these cars can take.

Both are original "D" cars built at the Jaguar factory, but in recent years they've led totally different lives. The first car is a nut and bolt, frame-off restoration, which would be used "lightly" at best. The second is still raced (in a friendly manner, of course). While some of Cavallo's clients undoubtedly have an abundance of money, nobody wants to stuff a D-type in a ditch through overexuberant driving.

The shop is, however, just overflowing with racing spirit . . .

Ultimately this is the area where the difference in the owners of exotic Euro cars really shows. The racer loves to drive, and views the risk of accident damage as an acceptable part of enjoying the car to its fullest potential. The concours owner is more driven by the pursuit of visual perfection. The worry involved in driving their immaculate car—and taking the risk of even the slightest damage—often results in a car that is not used at all, making the two camps as far apart as can be.

Shops like Cavallo are intimately familiar with the two directions exotic car ownership takes. They cater to both types of customer on a daily basis, so they're more familiar than most with the biggest divide in the automotive scene.

The shop is, however, just overflowing with racing spirit, and so they do lean slightly in that direction. This isn't to put down the concours mentality one iota—they do build some of the best show cars in the country—it just means that if you own an exotic European car, you just discovered a great new race shop.

Chequered Flag International, Inc.

Tim Bird

4128 Lincoln Boulevard

Marina del Rey, California 90292

310-827-8665

tim@chequeredflag.com

It's not uncommon to hear classic car enthusiasts explain that one of the things that makes a classic so special and so individual is that, unlike a new car, you can't just walk into a showroom and buy it in the color of your choice. As a rule, finding the perfect classic European car means putting in a lot of research.

A shop like Chequered Flag proves there can be an exception to that rule. With around 120 vintage and classic cars between their indoor showroom and outside parking lot, there's going to be something you want. Maybe you're searching for a Jaguar XKE? They often have four or five to choose from, in a variety of colors and ages.

Chequered Flag is based in Marina Del Ray, just a few miles from Los Angeles International Airport and only a few minutes from the beach. They are primarily a sales operation, owning most of their inventory. What this means to a buyer is that if they've seen something on their website, it will actually be there in the showroom. It's the kind of place you could go looking for a vintage Volkswagen and leave with a vintage Porsche—potentially dangerous if you love cars.

The owners and employees are all very professional. They will only offer help should you need them, the ultimate "no pressure" environment. Or it would be if it weren't for all those cars. Everywhere you look, you spy another saying, "Check out my curves. Take me home!"

The store sells classic American cars as well as the European stuff, but irrespective of where the cars were made, they all have one thing in common: originality. For Chequered to be interested in buying a vehicle for their inventory, it needs to be painfully original, usually with supporting documentation or original black Californian license plates. Quite simply that's what the majority of the market looks for in a high-end classic car.

As a rule, finding the perfect classic European car means putting in a lot of research.

The store sells classic American cars as well as the European stuff . . .

The type of cars can then be further broken down into either barn finds or good quality restorations back to original factory specifications. The "barn find" vehicles refer to cars which have usually been in the possession of very few owners since the vehicle was brand new, thereby not only avoiding restoration, but also the neglect and decay that warrants a restoration.

This kind of car will often have its original factory paint, and therefore have a beautiful aged look: a patina. The cars are most commonly known as "survivors" and have an extremely passionate following, particularly among Europeans.

Chequered Flag finds that most of their survivors are sold to European customers and shipped back "home." International sales are a large part of their business. Customers range from somebody who has specially come from Dubai to buy cars through somebody who just walked in off the street, to the biggest players from Hollywood, looking for a new toy.

Whoever they are, they won't be disappointed.

Corfee Car Care

Eric B. Corfee

2401 Manning Street

Sacramento, California 95815

916-649-0222

Italian supercars are quite different from most other vehicles in production. Firstly, they're usually built in very small quantities. Secondly, for most people they're prohibitively expensive to buy. Finally, sky-high insurance premiums and repair costs to keep one road legal and road worthy mean their owners have a never-ending incentive to keep bringing home the bacon.

So why do so many people fall head over heels for them? That's a hard one to answer from an objective standpoint. Not owning one of these cars makes it hard to relate to the emotions that drive the people who do. That pinpoints the only thing us outsiders can figure out: their ownership experience seems to be emotionally driven.

Nobody just "likes" his or her Ferrari. A Ferrari owner will sit in their garage looking at their beloved ride for hours on end. They won't fire up the engine while grooving to their iPod (and waste the sound of that lovely exhaust note?) and they certainly won't leave takeout food packaging sitting on their soft leather seats overnight. (This is not a Honda Civic, after all.) That these cars steal attention and deserve respect is quite apparent.

A Ferrari owner will sit in their garage looking at their beloved ride for hours on end.

The love which bonds the owners of these cars is also present in the people who've chosen to work on them. Sometimes this results in a Ferrari mechanic so immersed in the alternative universe that is Ferrari that they forget how things are to non-supercar-owning members of the public.

In the Sacramento area of northern California is an unusual Ferrari specialist named Eric Corfee who owns a business called Corfee Car Care. What makes Eric Corfee stand out is that—though he owns a Ferrari himself and can wax lyrical about the driving experience, about the addictive engine howl and the track-day rush—he's also got a natural ability to detach himself and see things from an outsider's perspective.

His knack is in helping these outsiders understand what it is to be an insider, without sugarcoating things. "We all grew up with James Bond," he says, "and that's where these cars come from. And no matter how they're put together or who puts them together, or how they've been repaired or how they haven't been repaired, you definitely want a piece of it."

While he'll work on any Ferrari— from cars in current production right back to the front-engined classics—he says it's the modern generation of cars that have really shaken things up. Many of the older cars were primarily garage art, vehicles which only saw the occasional weekend drive (though recently they've become hard-driven track tools). The modern generation have become daily drivers because, quite simply, they're now good enough to take the punishment.

... it's the modern generation of cars that have really shaken things up.

"They're it, they're the reference point. The mid-engined Ferraris are very user friendly. You could put just about anybody in one of the newer Ferraris, send them out on the track, and by the end of the day they'll not only be doing things they never thought possible, but they'll be doing things that are just flat out fun."

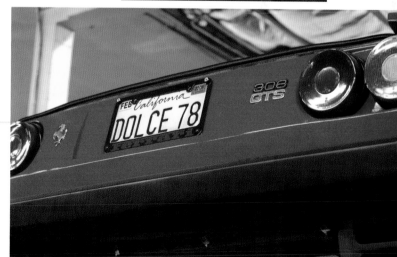

This new dynamic has changed the type of customers he typically sees, and he's enjoying this new variety. He'll explain that yes, the overall maintenance and repair costs are still higher than with most vehicles, but driving these cars on a track is now unlikely to result in any expensive repairs. It's even resulted in him taking part on track days with his own car, which—after all these years of working on them—finally makes him feel like he understands one hundred percent of what the car is about. "It is the most fun an adult male human being, or female for that matter, can have without going to jail!"

Now that sounds like something we non-Ferrari owners can relate to!

Coventry Cars of San Diego

Trace Luckett, Bill O'Brien

5097 Santa Fe Street

San Diego, California 92109

619-297-9393

Most of the automotive manufacturing in Britain took place in one region. Such centralized manufacturing is common: think Detroit in the U.S., or northern Italy for Italian cars. In Britain that region was the Midlands, an area circled around the country's second largest city, Birmingham.

This area was home to Land Rover, British Leyland (which ultimately included MG, Triumph, Morris, Austin, Rover, and Mini) plus motorcycle legends such as Norton, Triumph Motorcycles (a separate company from British Leyland's Triumph cars), and BSA. It was also home to Jaguar, which built cars in Coventry, a city just outside Birmingham.

Back in Britain, Jaguars (more commonly known as Jags) were a wealthy person's car. This was not so much due to the initial purchase cost—it had more to do with the price of gas. By British standards, the big cats really drank the stuff. In the U.S., the price of gas has usually varied from a quarter to a third of what the Brits pay per gallon. So predictably enough, lots of Jags were sold in America, most of them in California.

In the San Diego area, there is one Jaguar workshop that everyone recommends, Coventry Cars of San Diego. This business is owned by Bill O'Brien and Trace Luckett, both of whom have been in the auto business for 34 years. Hopefully, the name of their company should now make perfect sense.

The cars from Coventry are the only brand they'll work on, but they'll work on anything built by them. From vintage XK120s through XKEs and Mark IIs to the latest of the breed, Bill is fond of saying "We'll do anything on any Jaguar." They're so focused on Jaguar that it's actually very rare to see anything else within their workshops. Sometimes they'll fix a customer's Rover or Aston Martin, but only if the vehicle's owner is already one of their regular Jag customers.

The cars from Coventry are the only brand they'll work on . . .

The cars start coming into Coventry Cars the second they're out of their factory warranty, usually finding the shop by recommendation. And once people start using the shop, they stay. As with many specialist shops, some of the work is sent out to other trusted local businesses, like body, paint, upholstery, and rebuilding transmissions, but everything else is done in their own workshops.

Bill has noticed over the years that Jaguar fans are a fiercely loyal bunch. Most of his customers are more than just repeat customers, they're also longtime Jag owners. Even if they've had a car with a problem, it never seems to stop them from replacing it with another Jag.

So considering that he lives with Jags all day, every day, is he infected with the obsession too?

Apparently not, though he used to be. The many years of spending 60 to 70 hours per week living and breathing Jags means that he's ready for a rest at the end of the day. A few years ago he traded in his own big cat for another big animal—a horse. Now he owns five of these graceful animals, to which the average Brit would undoubtedly say, "If you thought a Jaguar was expensive to run . . ."

In the San Diego area, there is one Jaguar workshop that everyone recommends . . .

Darrin's MG Service

Darrin M. Sher

9318 Oso Avenue., Unit G

Chatsworth, California 91311

818-882-4414

Chatsworth is a small Californian town about forty-five minutes from downtown Los Angeles. The area remained rural, complete with tumbleweed and a typically western appearance, until around twenty-five years ago. As a result it was often used by the TV and movie industry as a Wild West location for all sorts of cowboy films.

In the eighties the town started to see development and modernization. One of the town's new businesses was created by a young car enthusiast fresh out of college named Darrin Sher. Darrin had played with engines since he was a kid, starting with go karts and mini bikes. By the eighties he'd already made a name for himself by knowing his way around every nut and bolt of an MG.

His love for all things MG started when his mother bought an MGB that became his when he turned sixteen. He drove his beloved MG during college. Everywhere he went other MG owners would stop him to ask where he got it fixed. Darrin could only answer by explaining that he was his own MG mechanic. As this was around the time that the official MG service chain was closing, Darrin would pick these folks up as his own customers, one after another.

It snowballed into a real business and that's how, twenty-six years ago, Darrin found himself opening his own MG repair shop in Chatsworth, California. His shop is still going strong, so much so that he always has a list of people ready and waiting to bring their cars in for work.

Darrin has always stayed faithful to the MG brand, and has therefore developed an incredible depth of knowledge on these cars—this explains his rock-solid reputation. If you own an MG in the greater Los Angeles area, you go to Darrin's. Some people go in when there's something wrong with their car, others when it needs a service, but many go in when their poor old MG is just showing its age. Whether it's a concours quality restoration, a bit of rejuvenation, or even some engineering improvements, Darrin's MG Service does it all.

Amazingly, he still owns his first car, that MGB he drove to college.

They're currently developing their own high capacity radiator for the classic MGs, a radiator that will finally put an end to the overheating problems that plague MGs which live in hot climates. He's also cured another one of the inherent MG flaws: by using a modern Bosch alternator in place of the old-style Lucas, he can rapidly fix the worst of the cars' electrical issues. To him, it's just another step in giving these beautiful old cars some modern-car usability.

Though occasionally a regular customer may bring in a different British sports car, MGs are still Darrin Sher's true passion. Amazingly, he still owns his first car, that MGB he drove to college. He's also collected some other MGs along the way (and modern cars too, including a Mini Cooper).

Thanks to his knowledge he can still enjoy driving his old MGs. And thankfully, because of his business, so can plenty of other car enthusiasts in the Los Angeles area.

Darrin had played with engines since he was a kid . . .

DeLorean One

Edward R. Bernstein

20229 Nordhoff Street

Chatsworth, California 91311

818-341-1796

If you're not a DeLorean aficionado, you may have never realized that these unusual sports cars were in fact European-built, therefore warranting a place in this book. Most of us are aware that the company's founder, John DeLorean, was an American, and that the cars were made for the American market—but that's about the extent of most people's knowledge of the brand.

The cars were put together just outside Belfast in Northern Ireland. As for the founder, even before the birth of the DeLorean Motor Company, John DeLorean was already well known within the automotive industry. He played an important role in creating the Pontiac GTO, and therefore the birth of the whole muscle car genre. Unfortunately his DeLorean car venture suffered many problems, all of which have been covered in comprehensive detail in many other publications.

What's relevant here is that around 8,600 of his DMC-12 cars were made, of which 6,500 are estimated to still survive. It's not a bad survival rate for a car from the early eighties, due in no small part to the corrosion resistant nature of the vehicle's fiberglass and stainless steel construction.

The cars were put together just outside Belfast in Northern Ireland.

Even with all of the above information, it's somehow still surprising to happen upon DeLorean One in Chatsworth, California. As you approach the open doors of their specialist workshop, you can see a couple of DeLoreans inside. As you get closer you realize that it's more like five or six of them, no—make that ten or eleven. For most of us, that's the most we'll ever see in one place.

The enthusiasm of DeLorean One's owner, Ed Bernstein, is incredibly infectious, especially when he explains how his own personal car—a car he bought new—currently has 497,000 miles on it and is still going strong. He has raced the car many times, even completing the legendary Cannonball Run twice. He's also the proud owner of what he describes as the world's fastest DeLorean motor. Ed lives for DeLoreans!

Regarding the basic car design, Ed explains that there were some teething problems when the car was new (like any new car model) but it's all easily-fixed stuff. In his experience, anyone saying that a DeLorean is a car plagued by problems is somebody that simply doesn't know DeLoreans.

The enthusiasm of DeLorean One's owner,
Ed Bernstein, is incredibly infectious . . .

Ed's customers range from locals who bring their cars in for an oil change to enthusiasts from every country with a name you can pronounce. These people will often have their cars shipped to his California workshop for a full restoration, which can take up to eighteen months. Then they're carefully shipped back across the oceans to their delighted owners. Impressively, there's no shortage of customers willing to ship their cars to him from halfway across the world.

A good example of the commitment DeLorean One has to these cars is visible in their car hauler. Ed basically had a trailer built around two DeLoreans. The vehicles being transported are driven in and then strapped down: in the worst case scenario (if the trailer rolled over in an accident), on opening the doors you would find two perfectly protected DeLoreans suspended from the roof of the trailer.

So, while it may have been surprising to learn that DeLoreans are European cars—and even that there's a business devoted solely to keeping these cars in tip-top original condition—it shouldn't be any surprise that this business is located in car-crazy California.

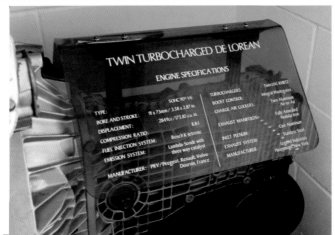

Dennis Sherman Foreign Car Service

Ray Beck

8620 La Mesa Boulevard

La Mesa, California 91941

619-464-7222

Just before World War II, Ferdinand Porsche was commissioned to design an affordable car for the masses. The result of this project was the "Volkswagen," translated as "people's car." That first model of VW would later become more commonly known as the Beetle.

Volkswagen survived the war by building a couple of military vehicles, both loosely based around the Beetle. At the end of the war, the factory was seized by the British, who miraculously kept it running. The commanding officers in charge of babysitting VW apparently never thought the cars would amount to much, as they not only looked very different from all other cars of the era, they were also mechanically very unusual.

Fast forward to the late fifties/early sixties and Volkswagen was still going strong, having steadily improved the Beetle. They'd also added a van and a sports car to their range. Against all odds, the vehicles found fans the world over. Ultimately Volkswagen ended up selling over 50 million Beetles worldwide, before retiring their air-cooled cars and redesigning their product range.

In the U.S., California was the Beetle state. The humble VW was an affordable little car that encouraged a generation to look beyond domestically-built vehicles, often sparking a love affair with European cars in general. Nowhere was this more true than in San Diego.

The old VWs are far less common now, as they've gone from being daily transport to valued classics. But many of the original Beetle owners still drive new-generation Volkswagens, while others drifted into owning Porsches, Audis, and BMWs. As the owners have moved into the newer style of German cars, so have the workshops, places like Dennis Sherman Foreign Car Service.

Dennis Sherman is based in La Mesa, just outside San Diego, and specializes in the aforementioned German cars. With Volkswagens they will only go as far back as working on the early water-cooled cars, though there are still a few classic air-cooled VWs hanging around that are owned by the proprietor.

On modern German vehicles, Sherman's does all the necessary mechanical work, including oil changes, brake work, suspension, electrical, plus engine and transmission repairs and overhauls.

You may have noticed in the accompanying photos that this particular shop contains newer German cars than most shops. That's because they're one of a small number of workshops whose customers are happy to have them work on cars still under warranty.

Volkswagen survived the war by building a couple of military vehicles . . .

To do this, the shop maintains a very good rapport with the local dealerships and must help their customers understand which items have to be done by the dealer to avoid potential warranty issues. Put simply, the service at this shop is so good that most locals want Sherman's to do as much of the work as they possibly can.

Considering all of the above, it's extremely impressive to learn that Sherman's hasn't advertised since the seventies and that all of their business comes from repeat customers or word of mouth. Shops like Dennis Sherman would serve as great models in business school.

On that subject, Volkswagen themselves must be worthy of study in business school: without their early influence, there would be considerably fewer European cars on the roads of America and in the workshops of California.

Put simply, the service at this shop is so good . . .

Dieter's Independent Porsche

Steve Grosekemper

1633 Market Street

San Diego, California 92101

619-234-8106

Every workshop has a specialty: usually it starts with the car brands they favor, and some shops then further specialize in just the mechanical aspect, or the body aspect. Seldom do you find a shop where the specialty is tuning and performance: seldom do you find a shop like Dieter's.

Dieter's is based in the heart of downtown San Diego, just a few blocks up from the famous Gaslamp Quarter. They are an independent, specializing in BMW and Porsche. Shop foreman, Steve Grosekemper, estimates that the workshop's overall business is an even fifty/fifty split between the two car brands—but his personal workload is considerably more focused.

Steve is Dieter's in-house Porsche tuning expert. His specialty is the modification of street cars into street hot rods, something the shop has become well known for. There is apparently quite a large demand for this kind of work with Dieter's customer base of mostly middle-aged professionals, and it's not because they're into illegal street racing. It's all about the racetrack.

This area is one of the most active regions within the Porsche Club of America, and one of their most popular activities is the organized track day. Not only does the local chapter organize track days at five or six different racetracks, there are also other local clubs organizing more for the true addicts. That's where Steve comes in.

Seldom do you find a shop
where the specialty is
tuning and performance . . .

Any Porsche owner who becomes active in the local club quickly learns
that track days are just about the most fun you can have in your car.
They also notice that some other drivers are going faster than they are,
and one thing leads to another. Steve explains that the Porsche factory
builds cars for a compromise between power and economy, a balance
that can be adjusted to suit the owner's needs.

To get more power out of his customers' cars involves technical engine management work, using not only Porsche computers but Bosch computers too. Dieter's has computers capable of tuning cars from the early eighties right through to the present day, machines capable of dramatic results.

Steve uses a recently completed 911SC as an example. This is a car that was originally rated at 179 horsepower, and usually there's 15 percent less power at the rear wheels than the manufacturer's rated number. They just dynoed this particular car at 245 horsepower with a catalytic converter and stock exhausts still fitted—the car was even street and smog legal! This particular Dieter's customer now has a serious car for club track days, which is still road legal and practical. That's what most of them want.

. . . the car was even street and smog legal!

To add to the appeal of the work, Steve also has a reputation for getting a lot of power for the money, something that he takes great pride in since most of his customers are also his friends at the racetrack.

So, what does Dieter's foreman, Steve Grosekemper, drive? No surprises here: he has a 914-6

Porsche built to race, with a full tubular frame. He also owns an '83 911 Cabriolet that looks stock from the outside but wins most of the local Autocross events, even when pitted against setup coupes.

Steve clearly isn't tuning Porsches for the money: it's a labor of love, a fact that's certainly not lost on Dieter's army of loyal customers.

European Collectibles

Christopher Casler

1665 Babcock Street

Costa Mesa, California 92627

949-650-4718

europeancollectibles@pacbell.net

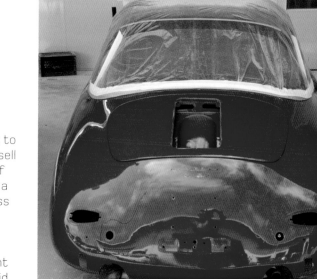

While the majority of specialist workshops exist to repair customer's cars, there are a few that sell a handful of cars—but they're in the minority. So if it's rare to find a specialist shop selling more than a few European cars, how rare is it to stumble across a place selling a hundred of them?

Walking through the front gate of European Collectibles for the first time is the adult equivalent of walking into Hamley's toy store in London as a kid. No, even better: it's the equivalent of walking from the Hamley's escalator onto the floor filled with just toy cars. You just don't know where to look: your eyes are in a hundred places at once.

European Collectibles has been selling and restoring cars since 1989. They concentrate on vehicles from the fifties and sixties—brands like Jaguar, Ferrari, MG, Austin-Healey, Aston Martin, and Mercedes-Benz—but for the last ten years they've specialized heavily in Porsche.

Their primary business is selling the cars, so their workshop only exists to aid in their sales operation. Practically, this means that if a customer wants to buy the green '67 Porsche 912, for example, they will make sure it is ready the way the customer wants it, on time for collection.

You just don't know where to look: your eyes are in a hundred places at once.

Some customers are after the unrestored, time-warp vehicle, and won't even want their "new old car" washed. Others only want the workshop to make their new purchase roadworthy.

European Collectibles

Many of their customers have been looking for a specific age, color, and spec for a long time, but want a mint car, which may not be what's in stock at European. In this case they can offer the customer their full restoration service.

It's quite common for a customer to go this route; the workshop will strip the car down to bare metal and rebuild it as new. They offer an impressive array of services in-house, even doing paint and bodywork. The only jobs sent out are upholstery and machine work, though in each case assembly and fitting are still handled back at European Collectibles.

One of the most impressive parts of this whole operation is that they can turn over enough cars to justify such enormous premises: like so many modern businesses, this is helped along by the Internet. Their website gets two thousand hits a day, plus they receive sixty emails, forty phone calls, and twenty people arriving in person to browse their extensive inventory. These are averages, but they show the impressive traffic that European gets.

Their website gets two thousand hits a day . . .

Since so many of their customers come via the Internet, many of the cars ultimately leave the state on completion of sale, and quite a large number of their cars even leave the country. It's understandable, as California is still known worldwide as the home of the rust-free classic car.

The only sad part of the internet sale is that so few of these customers will actually get to experience that sensation of childlike excitement as they first walk through the gates and see so many of their dream cars parked in the warm California sun.

European Sports Car Garage

Paul Lausevic

1929 16th Street

Sacramento, California 95814

916-441-5412

The people of Sacramento love their European cars, possibly more so than any other area. Almost every make imported into America is present on the town's streets: BMW, Mercedes-Benz, Saab, Porsche, Volvo, Jaguar, Volkswagen, and Audis—the cars are just everywhere.

Lots of European cars means lots of European car workshops: another one of the area's standout businesses is called European Sports Car Garage. This shop is operated by Paul Lausevic: he works in the automotive industry because he loves it. His father opened the business around forty-five years ago, and they've been at the same location since 1969 when this "new" building was erected as a replacement for the Art Deco building that originally occupied the spot.

Paul specializes in the upper-end European car brands mentioned above, but that's not how he initially got drawn to the business. His first love was old British sports cars: he still has his former daily-driver, a '73 Triumph TR6. More by accident than plan, it's been on one of the shop's lifts for a while now, due to the lead-free modern fuel gradually causing damage in its cylinder head. It's not a major problem, but it keeps getting harder for him to find time to put the old girl back together.

In years gone by, the European Sports Car Garage had fourteen people working. This was back in the days of the original Jags, Triumphs, and MGs. The cars were fairly maintenance intensive: things like ignition points needed adjusting on a seemingly endless basis. Things have changed a lot since then: the modern generation of cars doesn't need as much maintenance. Now it's more a case of replacing complete parts as they cease to work. The result for his business is that there are now four employees instead of fourteen.

Paul has also witnessed other changes. Back in the day there were just two or three "over the top" performance cars, and everybody

Lots of European cars
means lots of European
car workshops . . .

who loved cars dreamed of
owning one. Now, he says, every
manufacturer has a powerful
car. For him the effect has been
that, while almost every car is now
very good, they're also a bit more
"samey" and there aren't as many
"over the top" vehicles to get so
wildly excited about.

The classic Euro cars are still out
there, but not in the quantities
seen previously. Paul has witnessed
a familiar Californian problem,
watching his favorite cars getting
snapped up by visitors from all
around the world. Fifteen years
ago he had a core group of
customers still using MGs and
Triumphs daily: now there are
barely any.

. . . the location of this warehouse will remain strictly private.

It's not something that causes him undue concern. He's still happily working on European cars, but now they're the newer breed of European performance sedan, rather than the old style of smaller sports cars. But the other reason he's not losing sleep is that a while ago, when the cars were more readily available, he bought enough to fill a warehouse . . .

Yes, you read that correctly, Paul bought a bunch of his favorite cars and has them stored away. There's no particular plan for them right now, they're "just there." Given some of the tales floating around about overenthusiastic classic and vintage car shoppers from overseas—and the fact that passionate locals are finding it hard to locate good classics—the location of this warehouse will remain strictly private.

Considering how much the people of Sacramento love their European cars, both modern and classic, the least we can all do is let them keep some of the cars for their own pleasure!

Francorchamps of America, Inc.

Rod Drew

935 Sunset Drive, Suite A

Costa Mesa, California 92627

949-631-6373

Some Californian workshops emphasize their customer-friendly showrooms, advertising that fact at every opportunity, always looking to bring in more foot traffic. Others are happy keeping a lower profile and try to keep people out of their dirty, busy workshops so they can concentrate on fixing their loyal customers' cars. There's another kind of workshop in California too, a very different kind: the shop that exists totally off the radar.

Francorchamps of America (FAI) is easy to miss. They're situated on a quiet back street of Costa Mesa, and that's how they like it. There's no sign on the street and the cars are always kept under covers whenever they're in the parking lot. This isn't the glossy showroom kind of business: it's a place you'll only discover if somebody deems you worthy of recommendation.

So what do they do here? They service and restore Ferraris. That's it. A couple of Lamborghinis are visible in the photos but, as FAI boss Rodney Drew says, "I got conned into doing a couple of Lamborghinis by customers who own Ferraris!"

The extent of their work is very impressive; they'll strip these supercars down to body shells and nuts and bolts. At the time of our photo shoot, there were six Italian supercar motors scattered throughout the workshop in pieces: two boxers, a 275 two cam, a 275 four cam, a Miura, and a Daytona—enough to give the average car mechanic a mental breakdown.

Most of the machine work on the motors is done in-house, and that's a rare thing. Though, when you're talking about complex engines from a high-strung Italian supercar, it's probably wiser to keep the engineering work under your own control. There's no room for error with these cars—the parts are too expensive.

There's no sign on the street and the cars are always kept under covers . . .

You have to remember that Ferraris are only ever built in small batches: these are a long way from a Fiat Cinquecento. Having everything originally made in small quantities could prove problematic at restoration time, but FAI is filled with old-school craftsmen: if a part isn't available, they'll make it. FAI's boss, Rod, is a relaxed and modest person, so when he says, "We can make or build just about anything you'd need for a car," you know to take him at his word.

Just a bunch of highly-skilled craftsmen quietly doing whatever is necessary.

Francorchamps of America, Inc.

So, there's no advertising, no sign, no cars visible from the street, no showroom, and no swanky waiting room for the customers. Just a bunch of highly-skilled craftsmen quietly doing whatever is necessary to bring these handmade supercars back to their former glory.

And that's the kind of shop this is: if you're one of L.A.'s movers and shakers, and you've picked up an old Ferrari that's looking tired, your people drive it to FAI and they restore it—no drama, no fanfare. For most of us, shops like this will only ever exist in the pages of a book, but somehow it's still great to know they're out there.

Frank's Automotive

Frank and Nick Lettini

5220 Folsom Boulevard

Sacramento, California 95819

916-452-0917

If you love your car, the prospect of finding a workshop that's knowledgeable and trustworthy enough to fix it can be intimidating. Anybody living in America who has chosen to buy a car of European manufacture has immediately stepped out of the mainstream, making the shop selection process even trickier.

Add to this the fact that almost any European car costs more than its domestic counterpart and you're left with the simple truth: as a European car owner, finding the right place can be downright daunting.

Picking the wrong place can result in shabby quality repairs (ultimately requiring more money to be thrown at the subsequent redo). Or, an unscrupulous place can use the fact that your car is of a performance-orientated nature and thus can be expected to have costlier parts, coming up with a repair bill equal to the value of the car.

The best way to avoid problems is to take a common sense approach to the job of selecting a shop. Firstly, if you love your car, look for a workshop that shares that love. Next, look for evidence that they are true experts in their field, and finally, stick to shops who've been doing business for a long, long time. If they've weathered the decades, it's because they haven't burned local bridges.

. . . as a European car owner, finding the right place can be downright daunting.

Take Frank's Automotive in Sacramento for example. As you walk into their workshop, you see a row of immaculate vintage Porsches—nothing screams love like a collection of vintage cars. Secondly, one of their cars is a race car, and you certainly can't put together a race car unless you know your stuff. Finally, the evidence is everywhere for the world to see—they've been around since '69, and Sacramento's a relatively small town.

In a joint like this, you can figure out what's what before you even talk to anybody.

It turns out that Frank's was established by a car nut called Frank and Lettini. In those early days, like many conscientious business owners, he would work all of the hours that God sent. It was very common for his wife to come in at night with their two young sons and, as Frank finished up and closed the shop down, she would change the kids and put them to sleep in the back of the family station wagon.

Frank loved his European cars so much back then that he drove a Porsche 914-6 as his daily driver and had a 356 modified for track use, plus he'd fix them all day and night as part of his work. Who'd have thunk that those two young boys would catch Dad's bug?

Firstly, if you love your car, look for a workshop that shares that love.

Fast forward to the present day: Frank's son, Nick, is a co-owner in the business. Things have changed a lot, but not unrecognizably so. Frank still has the 914-6 and an old racecar, plus '56 and '57 Porsche Speedsters, and a 911SC. His son Frank has his own '63 Porsche coupe too, plus a '63 Alfa Romeo Giulietta convertible. Meanwhile, the station wagons that young Nick used to nap in have become some of the most potent of modern road burners, and those are exactly the cars that they now work on.

From Audis and BMWs to Porsches and Mercedes, if it's German they know every square inch of it at Frank's. And with their family history, they'll happily fix the newest ones right through the old fifties air-cooled breed. This is their love and it has been for decades: exactly what you're looking for in a shop, right?

German Auto Center

Omid Kalantar

1800 Rosecrans Street

San Diego, California 92106

619-222-6711

Point Loma, just outside the city of San Diego, is a predominantly military area with a large percentage of the local population being either active or retired Naval workers.

The area is well known for having a village mentality. One example of this is the way residents pride themselves on loyalty to the local businesses. Nestled away in the foothills of the Point is one such business, a BMW and Mercedes specialist called German Auto Center.

The current owner is a gent named Omid Kalantar. He's the second generation of Kalantars at the helm, running things much the same way his father did since he started the shop in 1982.

The shop has always been at the same location, but there have been a few changes over the years. When German Auto started up, it specialized in the Porsches and VWs which were so numerous in southern California at the time. As local tastes evolved, they added BMW and Mercedes-Benz to the mix. Later on—as the electronic management systems of cars in general got more complex—Omid decided he needed to concentrate the expertise of his staff into a more manageable quantity of car brands, picking the two recently-added brands of BMW and Mercedes as his specialty.

The shop has always been at the same location,
but there have been a few changes over the years.

Now the shop is known as Point Loma's main independent
specialist in these vehicles, working on everything
from engine management systems to full transmission
rebuilds. The only things the shop doesn't do are the
generic fixes, such as bodywork or replacing tires.
Basically, once a local Mercedes or BMW is out of
warranty, its owners bring it to Omid's shop.

As Point Loma has such a village mentality, everybody
knows each other. This situation has the potential to be
good or bad, depending on how you behave. As Omid says,
"If you screw something up, everybody's going to hear
about it!" It obviously serves Omid well, as his customer
base is almost solely long-term repeat business.

German Auto Center

Over the years he's seen his customers get married and have kids. He's even watched the kids grow up.

And it's not just the customers who stay loyal: he's even had cars change hands locally, but still continue coming into his shop. This seems reminiscent of the VW Bug movie, Herbie, appropriately enough!

The years of working on these brands has taught Omid a lot about German cars. He's realized that the over-engineered bottom ends of most German car engines are almost indestructible, but the complex cylinder heads are more prone to problems and so end up being a reasonably common fix at his shop. In his words, the German cars "Are definitely more high performance, a little bit more expensive, and a lot more sensitive . . . That's why it's not Japanese Auto Center!"

Omid has had so many cars come through his workshops that he's learned which ones best suit his personal needs. Surprisingly, it's the cars from the eighties and nineties, not the classics or the brand-new models. He's noticed that the newest cars are somewhat over-engineered and the classics are always prone to parts issues, be it cost or just poor availability. So a few years ago, the expert settled on the "sweet spot" right in the middle.

If you live in Point Loma and drive a Mercedes or BMW, then it's quite likely that none of this is news, as you probably already go to German Auto Center. If you don't, then maybe you should—it can't be hard to find somebody local who'll give you a recommendation.

. . . he's even had cars change hands locally, but still continue coming into his shop.

Heritage Garage

Graham C. Reid

1701 Pomona Avenue.

Costa Mesa, California 92627

949-646-6404

A great variety of cars have come out of Europe over the decades, from rapid German saloon cars to handbuilt Italian supercars and compact, affordable British sports cars. None have carved their own niche as effectively as the original Mini.

In countries where urban congestion is a relentless reality and congested on-street parking is an evil necessity, the Mini made a whole lot of sense. In America it's often viewed with utter confusion—though apparently not always.

If you drive around Costa Mesa's car district for a while, you'll eventually stumble across Heritage Garage. You'll know when you're there, as they usually park a nicely-restored Mini in the middle of their open workshop doors—at a ninety-degree angle from the way any other car would fit. You can do that kind of thing in a Mini. In fact you can do a lot of things in a Mini, like beat a Corvette around a small twisty racetrack.

This is a point not lost on the folks at Heritage Garage. The owner, Graham Reid, has been in the automotive industry since his youth back in Scotland, where he worked for both Rolls-Royce and British Leyland. Since emigrating to America he has worked on Jaguars, Range Rovers, and Aston Martins, but ten years ago he decided to narrow the focus of his business to just the Mini.

None have carved their own niche as effectively as the original Mini.

Why Minis? A Mini was Graham's first car, which is quite common for anybody growing up in Britain. Like most other people, he fell in love with that Mini. The love never quite went away and now he not only runs his Mini business, he also races the dinky cars. Miraculously, you really can beat most cars around a short racetrack in a Mini. Its original designers understood how impressive horsepower figures are far less important than light weight, perfect balance, and great handling. And, as many annoyed vintage racers will tell you, Minis sure do handle.

Miraculously, you really can beat most cars around a short racetrack in a Mini.

This is an area where Graham's own personal experiences on the track have contributed to an improvement of the car in general. He's developed a handling kit for the classic Mini, consisting of a coil spring conversion (not the more common coil-over-shock) which he mates with specially-imported Brembo brake rotors, EBC Kevlar brake pads, and fully-adjustable Gaz shock absorbers. The results are dramatic, surprising the hell out of Mini owners who'd never dreamed their cars could go around corners any quicker.

There is now enough word of mouth about these conversions that Heritage fits two or three of their full handling kits a month. On top of these improvements they're also busy with a million other jobs, like servicing the little cars and even completing show-winning restorations using a rotisserie style body support.

When asked whether Mini owners have an eye on the end value of their car as they pay for a restoration, Graham explains that—while it's inevitably a consideration—it's not at the forefront of their mind. Mini owners are much more focused on the fun of driving their cars, which is apparently what Minis are all about.

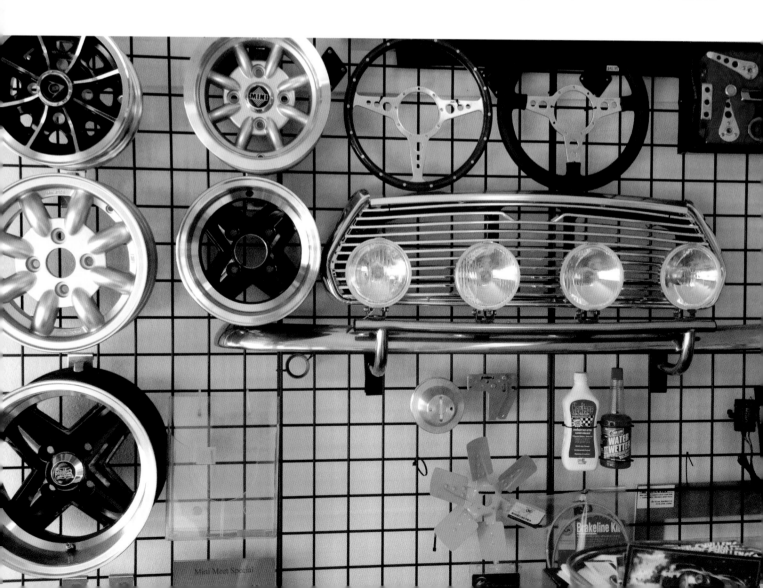

Ital Automotive and D'Mar Auto Repair

Joaquin Partida

4887 Voltaire Street

San Diego, California 92107

619-297-6620 Italian cars only

619-223-2434 All others

The country of Italy is responsible for creating some of the most beautifully-designed products in the world: from clothing to espresso machines, the way an object looks is paramount to most Italians.

It's therefore quite logical that so many car enthusiasts credit Italy with creating more works of automotive art than any other country. Even looking beyond Italy's legendary car manufacturing companies, there are also the world-famous design houses of Pininfarina and Zagato. Both companies design cars for a variety of automotive manufacturers, often from other countries. Italy is the home of great design.

When most of us visualize a beautifully-designed Italian car, we initially think of a supercar—a Ferrari, Maserati, or Lamborghini—but, as with most countries, there are different levels of vehicle on offer. While their supercars are symbols of national pride, they're also something that most Italians are unlikely to own. That's where the other Italian carmakers come in: Alfa Romeo, Fiat, and Lancia.

These other Italian car manufacturers have always made cars which are considerably more affordable to buy and to run, yet lack none of the dramatic design cues or racetrack-ready handling capabilities of their bigger brothers.

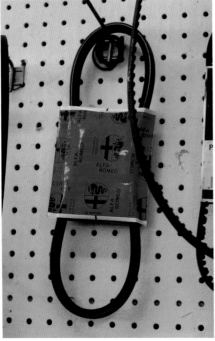

As with so many other European cars from the fifties through to the seventies, these affordable Italian sports cars were particularly popular in California. Unfortunately, because of southern California's legendarily rust-free climate, their numbers steadily dwindled, as visiting car enthusiasts bought them up and shipped them back overseas.

. . . the way an object looks is paramount to most Italians.

Disappearing cars isn't a new phenomenon in San Diego, but for some reason it turned out much worse for the affordable Italian cars than any other kind of vehicle. So much so that there are very few cars left, and only one remaining local repair shop: Ital Automotive.

Ital Automotive was founded by a gentleman named Carlos Platt. Carlos has been in this business for thirty-seven years, though this Ocean Beach location is new. Being in business for so long means

he's doing something right, and he appreciates that his survival has ultimately been due to keeping his customers. "My customers follow me. Most of my customers are old customers, meaning they've been coming to me five, ten, fifteen, twenty, thirty years."

Over that period of time he's watched things change. "There's not many autos left, and the other people that were in business, they've closed down." This situation has left Ital Automotive as San Diego's only remaining specialist.

As he is the only shop, he makes sure to offer everything an owner could ever want for their car, from full restoration through refurbishment to general service needs. He'll even happily take on performance modifications, though California's laws restrict that to vehicles from 1974 or older. Ital Automotive also sells parts for Italian cars, so any local owner wanting to do the basics at home can still come in to the workshop, even if only to buy the bits they need.

Being in business for so long means he's doing something right . . .

Carlos has an employee who will work on the other miscellaneous vehicles that come into the shop. But Carlos himself only works on the Italian cars: considering that he's the last of the breed, he doesn't really need to work on anything other than the area's remaining Alfa Romeos, Fiats, and Lancias.

It seems a real shame that the appreciation of these beautifully-designed Italian cars almost led to draining the entire area of their existence.

Postscript: After visiting Ital Automotive, the business changed hands and combined with D'Mar Auto Repair, now owned by Joaquin Partida. However, the one shop remains divided right down the middle – Italian cars on the one side, others on the other!

La Jolla Independent

Carl Nelson

5535 La Jolla Boulevard

La Jolla, California 92037

858-488-1555

carl@bimmerdoc.com

La Jolla is a very upmarket neighborhood: it's something you're aware off the second you drive into the area. Towns like La Jolla never seem to have factories, water treatment areas, or highways running through them. Towns like La Jolla never seem to have old-fashioned busy car repair shops either. But, amazingly enough, there is at least one here.

Nestled right in the heart of the town is a workshop with so many cars crammed into their lot that the doors almost touch, a place that positively overflows with old car parts. The business is called La Jolla Independent and its owner, Carl Nelson, is aware of the unlikeliness of their continued existence is such a neighborhood. He smiles as he explains how some residents are not "overly pleased" by their existence.

Carl is a true expert in the field of BMWs. In fact, he's the service advisor for the BMW Car Club of America. His La Jolla business concentrates solely on BMW cars, from the fifties right through to the present day. The shop will undertake any mechanical work and full restoration work too, but that's not what makes them unique.

La Jolla Independent

A while ago, La Jolla Independent started offering a neat conversion to the owners of classic BMWs. It has turned out to be very popular, particularly with the owners of the beautiful 2002 models. In layman's terms they're offering an engine conversion, among other things. They will fit a late model engine of the same family into an older car. As the mechanical lineage is there, all of the brackets match up perfectly.

A typical car would receive a modern, fuel injected 2.5-liter motor, producing 207 ft lb of torque, with a flat torque curve: the power is constant from 1900 to 5800 rpm. The swap also gives the car around 200 rear wheel horsepower and great fuel economy—but it gets better.

Carl's conversion is carefully set up so that the owner can go into any decent BMW shop, anywhere in the world, and they're able to plug in their standard BMW diagnostic equipment. Therefore any shop is able to analyze problems as if it were a factory-built car. Considering Carl's already had cars shipped to him from the east coast of the U.S., Hawaii, and even New Zealand, it's a genuinely useful benefit.

Also, his conversions are clean, like California clean. The emissions coming out of the tailpipe of one of his converted 2002s were so clean that he was getting better readings without a catalytic than the modern donor vehicle achieved with a cat fitted.

On top of this, Carl's business also operates the most comprehensive parts shop on the planet for classic BMW cars. Their reputation knows no bounds, especially for the E9 CS type BMWs and the 2002 models. They're literally shipping bits to every remote part of the planet on a daily basis. All of this work, and Carl and his employees even manage to have fun doing it. As he says, "We have a great time. I just wish we had more time!"

So while La Jolla may not be the kind of neighborhood you'd expect to stumble across a shop like this, the local folks should be proud of it. La Jolla Independent is taking beautiful, classic BMWs—the kind of collectible cars favored by the local residents—and making them as clean environmentally as a brand new BMW model. What could be more Californian than that?

They're literally shipping bits to every remote part of the planet on a daily basis.

Land Rover Specialists

3770 Hancock Street

San Diego, California 92110

(619) 298-9020

San Diego's passion for European cars isn't restricted to the vintage and classic variety. Many locals used to have a real love affair with British sports cars, but Triumph, MG, Jensen, and Austin-Healey all went out of business. At exactly the same time that people stopped driving those now-classic Brit cars, the nationwide SUV craze started to take off. So perhaps it's not surprising that San Diego now has such a large quantity of Land Rovers.

Land Rovers may be a long way from MGBs and TR6s, but they're still unmistakably British. They're built with some thought to real world physical proportions and they're designed to give the owner some driving pleasure, unlike so many other modern behemoths. Basically they're still sporty when compared to their domestic equivalents, just like the cars from so many years before.

As with so many new cars, Land Rover owners are pretty tied to the franchised dealerships for their service and repair needs for at least the first couple of years. After that they're free to shop around.

At the top of the list for independent Land Rover repair shops in the San Diego area is a place called Land Rover Specialists.

Here they'll work on all Land Rover vehicles, from the common Discovery and Range Rover to the rare Defender. If you're reading this book elsewhere in the world, the Defender is probably your most common model of Land Rover. Unfortunately, in the U.S., the ultimate do-anything, go-anywhere workhorse was only imported in tiny quantities.

The head man at Land Rover Specialists is an Englishman called Ian Gill: being from the vehicle's birthplace, he knows his Brit cars inside out.

He didn't always run a Land Rover-only workshop: he used to distribute his time more evenly among all British vehicles, doing everything from engine rebuilds to full restorations. In fact, the business is still officially listed as British Auto Repair, though it's now doing business as Land Rover Specialists.

As his Land Rover business has grown, he's found it ever harder to fit in the time required to fully restore an old sports car. He knows that a top-notch restoration can take anything from a year to eighteen months to complete, usually being fitted in around the day-to-day "emergencies." Thus, restoration is no longer a service that he promotes—but that's not to say it doesn't happen.

At the time of our photo shoot, he was working on an Austin-Healey from Mexico, and a Triumph TR3 that he describes as more refurbishment than restoration. He'll still work on anything British from the dawn of time up until around 1990: after that year, he sticks to Land Rover products only. Modern electronics (and the super-expensive diagnostic equipment necessary to fix them) force most privately-owned businesses to pick just one brand as their direction.

The love of British cars is obvious in this workshop: there's English-themed memorabilia scattered throughout the shop, and Ian's right-hand man still drives an MG to work most days.

As for Ian, his preferred form of transport sits behind the parts counter; it surprises most people as it's got two wheels and pedals. It shouldn't though, as it's the future for most cities. Going from MG Midgets to Hummers was never destined to last. Maybe Ian's just ahead of the curve.

. . . being from the vehicle's birthplace, he knows his Brit cars inside out . . .

Lanse's Auto Restoration

2261 Federal Avenue.

West Los Angeles, California 90064

310-473-0883

lh.auto@verizon.net

If you've ever been to Monterey and attended the Pebble Beach Concours d'Elegance then you'll be familiar with the standard of the entered vehicles. The cars displayed in the show are as close to automotive perfection as it gets.

But have you ever wondered what the journey of their restoration is like? What's the car like before the restoration? Who undertakes work of this standard?

They're all reasonable questions, and this business is one of the few places to find the answers. Lanse's Auto Restoration is a body shop in West Los Angeles, specializing in the collision repair and restoration of classic cars. Lanse's has been in this business since 1972, and, like most respectable businesses, they've seen steady growth over the years.

Right now there are seven employees working in this workshop, which is Lance's fourth location. Their core business is cars from the fifties, sixties and seventies, though they'll just as happily restore later-model Ferraris and Porsches. Most of their cars are brought in by regular customers—apparently it's very rare for them to work with somebody new without at least a referral.

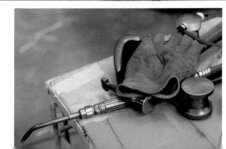

The customers themselves are either other local workshops, places that only do the mechanical side of the work, or L.A. car enthusiasts. The boss, Lanse Haselrig, explains that while there isn't really a typical customer—as regards age or occupation—there is a common thread that he sees in his repeat people. They almost always own six or seven collectible cars, either classics or newer sports cars, and they are very, very passionate about them.

Some customers may bring a car into Lanse's that's been in a fender bender, knowing that he's more than capable of bringing their Italian supercar back to as-new factory condition. Others may leave him a classic car that they'd like to have restored to the standard of an excellent daily driver, though there are a few customers who will bring in a car whose ultimate destiny is Pebble Beach.

Their core business is cars from the fifties, sixties and seventies . . .

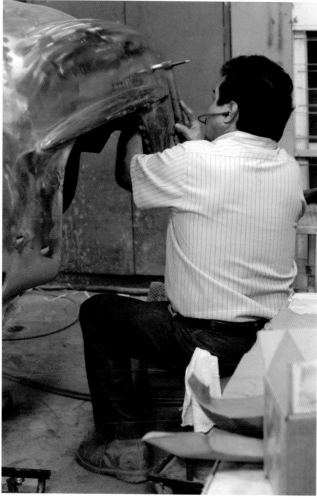

At the 2008 Pebble Beach Concours event there were several display cars that had previously been through Lanse Haselrig's workshop, which obviously makes Lanse very proud. It also shows that Lanse's Auto Restoration is far from new to this.

Most of their cars are brought in by regular customers.

These cars can start off in almost any condition, as this is one of very few shops willing to undertake anything body related. The missing body parts on the Aston Martin shown in the accompanying pictures make the car look like an intimidating repair to most car people, but not to him: "No, it's not intimidating to us. We're comfortable with full scale frame restoration: repairing frames, straightening frames, fabricating sheet metal pieces, aluminum, and steel. We don't have any problem with any of that stuff; we're pretty comfortable about repairing all of it."

So, as mind boggling as it may be to the rest of us, there's a high probability that the Aston Martin which looks so pitiful right now, may be taking home a Pebble Beach trophy at some point in the future. And now we've all been allowed a glimpse into one of California's private workshops that makes it all possible.

Laurence Anderson Co.

1214 Tenth Street

Berkeley, California 94710

510-527-2938

If you're the American owner of a European car, you probably care more about your vehicle than the average Joe. You appreciate its advanced design and beautiful build quality—and the performance that so often accompanies these cars is quite welcome too.

When European cars get older, the ownership experience gets a little more complicated. Classic European cars require more dedication on the owner's behalf—when you get to truly vintage European cars, you're entering a whole new world. The cars were made in a totally different era, on a continent thousands of miles away, making everything uncommon.

If this is you, then you already know that even a simple service can be fraught with complications: where do you find consumable parts like a set of contact breaker points?

This is Laurence Anderson's world: he runs a shop in Berkeley that specializes in rare and vintage European cars. Fifty percent of his customers' cars are early Rolls-Royce or Bentleys: "early" meaning pre-war—sometimes pre-WW I. The remainder of the cars that he works on are cars from continental Europe of a similar vintage.

To Laurence, each of these cars is like a giant jigsaw puzzle—a puzzle that's usually got some missing pieces. One of Laurence's most common tasks is to recreate parts which are no longer available so the owners of these cars can continue to use them.

there are examples of
steam train memorabilia
around his premises . . .

Obviously this type of vehicle isn't
driven on a daily basis: they're
used strictly for enjoyment, but
their owners do expect to be able
to use them.

Laurence explains that he must
put himself into the place of the
car's original designer (something
he's become quite adept at doing),
then research as much information
as is available before duplicating
the original part.

This is all fascinating stuff, but what's equally intriguing for any visitor to his shop is how his work has shaped his surroundings. If you're at all a visual person, then his workshop is a treat for the eyes. The research he has to undertake means ancient dusty motoring books line the shelves and benches. Mascots, road signs, and oddball parts are scattered throughout.

His love for these vintage cars has overflowed into other modes of transport from the era: there are examples of steam train memorabilia around his premises, even fully-functioning scale models of old locomotives.

Some of the cars in his shop are his own property too: it would be impossible for Laurence to do the work without sharing this passion for yesteryear with his customers. One car in Laurence's shop which stands out against the vintage backdrop is a classic '57 Alfa Romeo. "I do have a special soft spot in my heart for Alfa Romeo: I have a longstanding history with them and obviously ownership of the first series Sprint Veloce," he explains.

What's really special about his Alfa is something that often divides connoisseurs of old European autos: it's a survivor. This car has never been restored and even carries the original factory paint. This patina is something he appreciates immensely.

Really, it's an appreciation of the beauty within these old mechanical beasts that drives the man. He once rebuilt an AJS 7R motorcycle engine for one of his customers. This is noteworthy because Laurence does not ride motorcycles: the appeal of the rebuild wasn't related to a love of bikes, and it wasn't about earning the money. Laurence Anderson is quite simply fascinated by the engineering behind all classic and vintage forms of transport, whether they have two wheels, four, or many, many more.

When European cars get older, the ownership experience gets a little more complicated.

Liberty Motorsports

Jim Liberty

1638 Babcock Street, Suite F

Costa Mesa, California 92627

949-375-1888

jimliberty1@sbcglobal.net

Jim Liberty achieved great success working in real estate, enough that he was able to retire from this career early. That left him with a rather enviable decision: what to do next?

For Jim this was a no-brainer—real estate may have generated the income, but his first love had always been for early Porsche cars, in particular the 356. Retiring early simply meant that he could finally turn his love of restoring tired old examples into a business.

These days Jim owns and runs Liberty Motorsports where he restores Porsche 356s, one car at a time. Sometimes he'll add a second car but only if a holdup on one car would otherwise stop things completely.

Jim Liberty will only work with a certain kind of customer: they must understand the time commitment involved in restoring a car properly. They must understand the financial commitment. Finally (and most importantly) Jim only undertakes projects for the type of customer who is serious about their chosen restorer keeping an eye on every single detail.

Jim takes great pride in rebuilding these cars with a perfectionist's eye. His body man is an artist in every sense of the word. Born in Sweden, now living in California, this gentleman is a painter and sculptor, as well as a metal craftsman capable of handmaking any panel that is required for a car.

A good example is a '53 bent window coupe currently undergoing restoration. This car was located in New York and had an amount of corrosion throughout the body typical for a northeastern car. Jim estimates that around seventy percent of the body had to be recreated from almost nothing. The old panels were removed and used as a pattern. New panels were then stamped and formed with a planishing hammer, an English wheel, and dies that he makes in his own press.

Sometimes nine months of solid work go into the body before the car is sent out for painting. Once the car is completed, it is either returned to an ecstatic customer or put up for sale (if it is one of Liberty's own cars). Sometimes, if the car is a particularly rare or special example, Jim will add it to his personal collection, which currently consists of seven Porsche 356s.

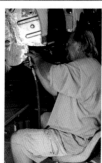

His body man is an artist in every sense of the word.

Jim takes great pride in rebuilding these cars with a perfectionist's eye.

What constitutes a special car to Jim can vary: it may be its age, meaning either a very early model or the last of a production run. He also has an affinity for sunroof cars—apparently almost all of his personally-owned cars have a factory-fitted sunroof.

Either way, once a completed car is sold or handed back to its owner, the next car is started.

Jim sums up his motivation for running Liberty Motorsports very succinctly: "At minimum I'd like to break even on them, and preferably make just enough to run the shop."

Lubo's Bavarian Motors

Ljubodrag "Lubo" Ljubisavljevic

3450 Elvas Avenue.

Sacramento, California 95819

916-451-5826

As you've been going through the various shops of this book, you've no doubt noticed a pattern: many people will buy their brand-new European car from their local franchised dealership, then get it serviced by the dealership at the intervals specified, but only while still within factory warranty.

At their first opportunity, most European car owners seem to run from the dealership like it's got the plague, on a mission to find themselves a good local independent specialist.

Another one of California's great independent workshops is Lubo's Bavarian Motors. If you know your BMWs then you'll have already figured out his specialty from the business name. If not, then today you'll learn something: Bavaria is the region in Germany where BMWs are built.

Ljubodrag Ljubisavljevic has been working on BMW cars for almost as long as he can remember. What's that? You're still hung up on his name? Yes, it's a mouthful for anybody not from the former country of Yugoslavia. A massive tongue twister the first few times you say it, it sounds incredibly easy to say when it comes out of Lubo's own mouth!

Lubo's Bavarian Motors

The big man knows we have a hard time pronouncing his first name, so he says, "Call me Lubo."

Lubo remembers first falling in love with Bimmers in 1969. Back then the now-classic 2002 model was being sold as the "Best Little Sedan in the World," a claim that Lubo was in full agreement with.

After the 2002 had been around for a few years, he picked himself up a beautiful low-mileage, one-owner example, which he still owns today. Now parked in his spotless reception area, it's really worth taking a look at. The car is still wearing its original paint: in fact, everything about the car is one hundred percent original.

. . . locally he is known as the one true expert on this particular make.

In the showroom he has a few other examples of what are, to him, examples of BMW excellence, both cars and motorcycles. One of his BMW-badged motorcycles is, by way of contrast, a motorcycle made in China for the Chinese Army. He bought this from a man in Hawaii, who had crated it up and shipped it there directly from China. What's interesting about the bike is the comparatively crude way in which it was manufactured.

The bike sits in Lubo's reception next to a German-made example, purely as a way of showing his customers the difference in quality.

While it's clear that Lubo is as big of a motorcycle enthusiast as he is for their cars, the shop is there just to service those cars from Bavaria. In his Sacramento workshop he'll work on most of the local BMWs which are out of factory warranty, but he'll also go right back in age to some of their most desirable classic models.

Lubo has multiple customers with cool oldies—classic 2002s and 2000CSs, even a Bavaria—though the majority of local cars are late models. To work on these cars, he has BMW's GT-1 computer, enabling him to tackle the most complex of computer issues. This is essential since computers are what make modern cars tick.

He explains that one of the most satisfying parts of his work is when a car comes in with diagnostic issues that were left unresolved by another workshop. For him, watching them drive away from his workshop, impressed and happy, is what makes it all worth it. It's also exactly what must keep his business so healthy: locally he is known as the one true expert on this particular make.

While having such a great local reputation undoubtedly makes the decision of which independent to go to in this area very easy, it must be maddeningly frustrating for the competition!

Lubo remembers first falling in love with Bimmers in 1969.

Marx Servicing Mercedes

Steve Marx

1950 Placentia Avenue.

Costa Mesa, California 92627

949-548-1153

Whether they're being used as a taxicab to Munich's Franz Josef Strauss airport or as a status symbol and accessory in Beverly Hills, Mercedes-Benz cars inspire fierce brand loyalty. One of Los Angeles' best-known independent Mercedes service shops is called Marx Servicing Mercedes, and is based in Costa Mesa—L.A.'s unofficial home of the specialist auto industry.

Marx's boss man, Steve Marx, started working on Mercedes when he was just fourteen years old. By the time he was eighteen he'd been moved up into a position where he ran the guy's shop. When he was twenty he figured it was time to have his own shop: that was thirty-seven years ago.

The whole time Marx has specialized in Mercedes and only Mercedes, which means that the variety comes from within the vehicles themselves. He's had everything in from a late-thirties 540K to the new stuff. Though the bulk of the work, he says, is in the 190, 230, 250, 280, and 300 SLs.

. . . Steve Marx, started working on Mercedes when he was just fourteen years old.

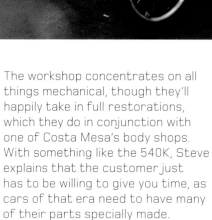

The workshop concentrates on all things mechanical, though they'll happily take in full restorations, which they do in conjunction with one of Costa Mesa's body shops. With something like the 540K, Steve explains that the customer just has to be willing to give you time, as cars of that era need to have many of their parts specially made.

153

Once the cars are completed, they're shipped all the way back to their homes again.

This is something they will happily dive into in-house. Steve's years of experience have shown him that it's much quicker to machine many of the odd parts yourself, than to wait for an overstretched machine shop to fit them in.

All of those years of experience within Marx's workshop have given them a formidable reputation, with cars coming in for work from all around the world. Off the top of his head, Steve Marx was able to remember specific cars which had been shipped to them from South Africa, South America, Japan, and even Germany for restoration work! Sending a car from the motherland to his shop in California is high praise indeed.

Once the cars are completed, they're shipped all the way back to their homes again. There are many businesses that'd do anything for that kind of reputation.

If you look at it from the customer's perspective, it also shows just how deeply these owners love their cars. Steve has learned that the "love affair" is the best analogy—to some of his customers, when they're looking at restoring their pride and joy, the attitude is "whatever it costs, it costs."

It's a mentality Steve can relate to, as it's obvious he has a love for the classic Benz: he even races his own classic Benz, regularly. That means he's firmly rooted in the built-to-be-driven sector of the car scene. This is fitting as Mercedes, more than so many other makes, really are built to be driven.

Cruising the nice neighborhoods of the Hollywood crowd while people admire you is one thing, but look at those German taxicabs—could there be a tougher life for an automobile?

Modern Classic Automotive

Jay Rapozo

1500 El Camino Avenue, Suite K

Sacramento, California 95815

916-920-5263

Fiats are uncommon cars on American soil, but there are a few specialists here and there. One such shop is Modern Classic Automotive in Sacramento.

Modern Classic was established by a gent called Leonard Rapozo: he first started working with Fiat cars at the dealership way back in 1968. In those early days, the hottest sellers were the little 850 models. Considering he'd been working on Fords immediately before that, these diminutive Italian cars must have seemed as different as oil and water.

The dealership where he was employed sold Fiat, Alfa Romeo, Peugeot, and GMC. He stayed at that dealership until it ran into trouble in '83. Leonard had planned to take over the Fiat part of dealership from the original owner but, as this was around the time that a decision was made to stop importing the cars into America, he quickly scratched that plan. He'd also considered opening a Lancia franchise, but back then the reputation of those cars had started to go downhill fast.

He opened up his own shop, Modern Classic Automotive, which turned out to be for the best. He really only wanted to work on Fiat cars, not to sell them, and this shop made that happen.

By '83 the most popular Fiats were the 124 Spiders. "The 124 Spider became popular because the body line was beautiful," Leonard recalls. They sold in very good numbers, especially when compared to any prior imported model.

Even though Fiat themselves had stopped bringing in the cars, Pininfarina continued bringing them in for another few years. This meant that a continuing supply of cars came in for service and repair work at Modern Classic. For the first few years, he remembers how his business was literally flooded with Fiats.

Over the decades, the amount of cars coming in has steadily dropped, which is no great surprise. Northern California has suffered the same problems as the southern part of the state. Not only is there the usual attrition rate due to accident damage, but also California has the added problem of vast numbers of vehicles being exported back to European countries by collectors eager to find a rust-free classic.

Now Fiats are the smallest part of Modern Classic's business, though once they were the largest. When Leonard opened the shop he set it up as a Fiat and domestic car specialist—now those domestic cars account for the bulk of the shop's business.

He really only wanted to work on Fiat cars . . .

These days Modern Classic Automotive is run by Leonard's sons, one of whom is the shop's sole remaining Fiat expert. "He knows them because he grew up with me," Leonard says.

Because of the rarity of the cars, it's actually become exciting for the guys at the shop to be able to work on one of the old Fiats. Though the quantities of local cars dwindled, their love for them never faded.

Any eagle-eyed Fiat fan will still be able to spot multiple rare parts scattered around the premises, ready to go onto the remaining local cars as needed. The Rapozo boys even have their own project 124 Spider out back, ready to be resurrected someday.

All they're left to do is reflect on how the affordable end of the Italian car business died. Popular opinion says that the last cars which came over were of such poor quality that the end was inevitable, a sad conclusion for some of the most exciting brand names in the automotive world.

Obviously, twenty years on, the cars being made currently by Fiat, Lancia, and Alfa Romeo are beautifully designed, solidly put together, and eminently desirable cars. They are cars that the Rapozo family would be proud to be associated with once more, though whether that will ever happen is, sadly, out of their hands.

. . . these diminutive Italian cars must have seemed as different as oil and water.

Monaco Motors

Wade Lennan

21311 Vanowen Street, #118

Canoga Park, California 91303

818-704-1836

Wade Lennan is in charge at Monaco Motors in Canoga Park, where they specialize in Mercedes-Benz, BMW, Porsche, and Ferrari. The majority of their business involves cars that are barely out of warranty, but in some cases it also includes cars still under warranty.

Legally you are able to have your car serviced away from franchised dealerships, and a great many of Monaco's customers have learned that there can be some very good reasons to do so. Wade recently had a customer come in with their car just out of warranty and a transmission that had to be completely rebuilt. In the case of this particular car, there was no scheduled maintenance required on the transmission for over 100,000 miles. So, even though the dealership had done everything required by the manufacturer, it wasn't enough.

In Wade's opinion some of the recommended service intervals are being stretched out too far, resulting in avoidable problems like this. Monaco has been around for many years, and their customers have learned from experience that listening to their service recommendations always leads to a longer-lasting car, rather than just rigidly sticking to the manufacturer's suggestions.

Wade's customers trust his judgment, and they're all enamored with the service they receive at this workshop. It's the kind of place where your car is collected from and returned to your home or office. It always comes back washed and vacuumed: they'll even buff out scuffs in the paintwork as a courtesy, a measure taken to keep their customers loyal. It works.

Aside from the maintenance on modern European cars, they'll sometimes launch into much more technical stuff when requested. Recently they fitted a 3.8 liter motor to a 2005 Porsche Boxster for a loyal customer who wanted

more power. What's most impressive is that the customer shipped the car to Monaco Motors and back from San Francisco, a 500 mile round trip.

Engine swaps on older vehicles are commonplace: hot rodders have been doing it for decades. It's always more interesting and challenging on a modern vehicle because of the space issues within the engine bay, and due to the complexity of the electronic management systems. That's where Monaco has another advantage, as they are one of only 500 Bosch Service Centers in the world.

Monaco Motors' core business is and always will be service...

they'll even buff
out scuffs in
the paintwork as
a courtesy . . .

In their workshop I found another example of the variety of work they'll undertake: among the computer-controlled late models was a classic Mercedes undergoing a slow-but-thorough restoration for another long-term customer. These aren't the sort of jobs that they advertise, but they'll do them none the less.

Monaco Motors' core business is and always will be service, but apparently what makes them stand out above the competition is a never-ending quest to provide the best customer service.

Moss Motors Ltd.

Giles Kenyon

440 Rutherford Street

Goleta, California 93117

1-800-667-7872

kenyong@mossmotors.com

Most of the specialist workshops in this book are invaluable to the car owners in their community. Without some of these shops, local owners would struggle to keep their beloved cars on the road. The key word in most of these cases? Local.

Moss Motors, as a business, has a much broader effect on the European car scene than most. Headquartered in Goleta, California, Moss isn't exactly reliant upon local business.

Moss Motors is one of the biggest classic car parts companies in existence. They specialize in British sports cars—meaning MG, Triumph, Austin-Healey, Mini and Jaguar—and their parts are shipped daily to owners in the most far-flung countries of the world.

The aim at Moss Motors is simple: to ensure availability of anything that's necessary to keep these old cars on the road indefinitely. Many of the relevant parts are already being manufactured by various specialist manufacturers, so Moss brings all of these existing parts together and itemizes them in their various catalogs. If a part is no longer available, then Moss will figure out how to make it available.

This might mean redesigning the part using their own in-house Research and Development department and then contracting out the actual manufacture. Sometimes it will even mean developing and manufacturing the part entirely in-house.

For the fun-loving crowd they developed a supercharger kit . . .

Not all of their parts are designed with originality in mind. While there are many classic British sports car owners who want a concours vehicle (exact replicas of what left the factory when new), there are plenty of others who own their cars primarily to drive them and have fun doing it. These owners often want go-fast parts. Moss caters to both.

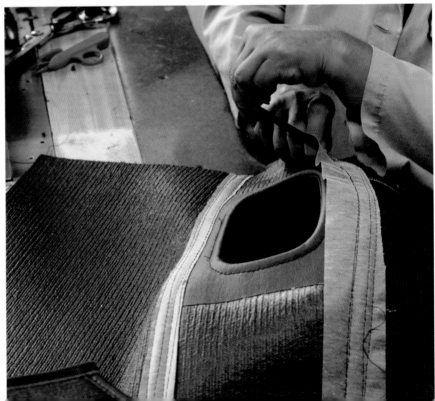

If a part is no longer available, then Moss will figure out how to make it available.

Take the Triumph TR6 for example. Many aficionados regard it as one of the best British-made driver's cars of the era. Jaguars may (arguably) outperform the TR, but they also come with much higher running costs. MGs may be just as affordable to run as the TR6, but they can't really match the Triumph's performance.

Moss's comprehensive parts catalog for the TR is fairly typical of the company's approach. For the originality crowd, Moss commissioned the production

of authentic, factory replica fuel pumps, correct down to the original style priming levers. For the fun-loving crowd they developed a supercharger kit, a bolt-on upgrade that can increase the rear wheel horsepower by a whopping fifty percent.

Moss also offers five-speed gearboxes, air conditioning systems, and brake rotors as effective as you'd find on any new vehicle, making their in-house R&D shop both their best-kept secret and most impressive asset. In the photographs you can see what's coming next: they're in the middle of developing a supercharger system for the earlier model Triumph TR3.

This kind of development is what makes Moss really stand out above the various other classic car parts specialists. It not only allows them to offer a more thorough product selection than their competition, it also extends the day-to-day drivability of these beautiful old British cars on today's challenging roads—something they aim to do forever.

Pacific International Auto

Jonathan G. Turner, III

1118 Garnet Avenue.

San Diego, California 92109

858-274-1920

jongt007@msn.com

Pacific Beach is an oceanside neighborhood of San Diego. It's just south of the respectable and affluent city of La Jolla, though the adjoining areas have very different flavors. Pacific Beach, locally referred to as PB, is predominantly occupied by a young college crowd. Most of its local retail consists of clothing and surf shops, bars, restaurants, and, let's not forget, one British car workshop.

Pacific International Auto is owned by a British car enthusiast named Jonathan Turner. He's aware that his shop isn't an obvious fit in the neighborhood, especially considering he's located on Garnet Avenue, one of the area's busiest hangout streets. But, odd as it may appear now, it wasn't always that way.

Jon initially got into cars as a kid. His father was a real Jaguar enthusiast (he owned an XK140) and, inevitably, Jon caught the bug from him. In high school, Jon got a job working for a local British car specialist and learned a lot about the business. When he finished his college education, he left to find there were no jobs. Considering where his passion lay, his best option was to open his own car business, Pacific International. This was back in 1975.

He's aware that his shop isn't an obvious fit in the neighborhood . . .

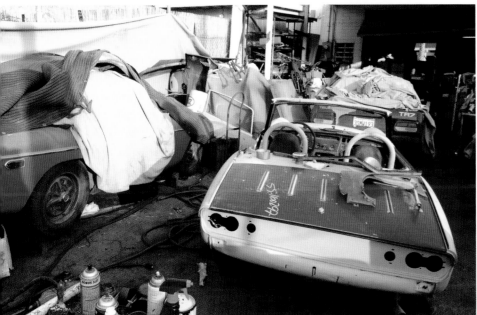

He's always specialized in Jaguar, MG, and Triumph, because they're his favorites. For a while he worked on a lot of Rolls-Royces as well. He'd always known they were the most technologically advanced of the British makes and that fascinated him, but he eventually decided to go back to his original three.

He's seen many things change over the years—more than just his PB location. When he started the shop his priority was sales, but he had to adapt quickly as the service work grew. As the cars grew older, major repairs became more common.

Eventually the cars started to look old too: that's how restorations became commonplace. Jon has always found restorations rewarding, as for him, returning the cars back to their original beauty makes all of the hard work worth it.

In the last ten tears or so, things have shifted again. With the growth of the Internet came a wider audience for most businesses—in his case it turned into a huge increase in the worldwide sales of parts. He laughs as he explains how he's still slowly getting rid of thirty years worth of junk.

He's always specialized in Jaguar, MG, and Triumph, because they're his favorites.

After all of these years being so closely involved with British cars, Jon still hasn't lost his own passion for them: he currently owns a Jaguar XKE and an XK120, plus an MGB and a couple of classic Volvos. Unlike many other shop owners, he still drives them to work every day. Perhaps that's the secret to maintaining your enthusiasm—the cars have always been about the driving experience.

There used to be other British car workshops in the Pacific Beach area, but over the years they've all disappeared. Jonathan finds it both amusing and odd that he's now located next door to a tattoo shop, the most recent in a never-ending series of changes in the businesses up and down Garnet Avenue.

Pacific International may initially look out of place amongst the tattoo parlors, surf shops, and bars of Garnet AveAvenuesue, but closer attention reveals the kids walking by his shop oohing and aahing at those cool old British cars. Now, if they could just get behind the wheel of one, the love for these cars would spread to the next generation.

Patrick Ottis Company

1220 Tenth Street

Berkeley, California 94710

510-849-3553

In a quiet backstreet in Berkeley is a row of garage doors. If it weren't for their size, they could easily pass as privately-owned storage garages, though being two or three times the size of a domestic garage door, there's a suspicion that something else lurks behind them.

Look more closely and there is a small sign next to a pedestrian doorway with Patrick Ottis Company printed on it. Knocking and then walking through this doorway is almost certainly going to result in surprise, as inside is a beautifully laid out workshop filled with exotic dream cars. You'd certainly never expect it from the outside: maybe that's the point.

Patrick Ottis is the owner of this business: he specializes in Ferraris, and only Ferraris. He's uncommon in that he really does stick to the one type of car, never being tempted to stray. He first started out with the Italian cars back in 1972, when he worked on the vehicles in both Oklahoma and Colorado, before relocating to the San Francisco bay area. His move to the northern Californian city was spurred on by a job at another Ferrari specialist: this one was a dealership that also had its own restoration facility. Apparently, this was the first restoration shop in the U.S. designed around repairing historic racing cars.

He's uncommon in that he really does stick to the one type of car . . .

Now Patrick Ottis runs his own company, employing four very skilled Ferrari experts. His workshop concentrates on the mechanical aspects of the cars only—particularly on vehicles built in the fifties and sixties.

Though an incredibly niche market, it's one that works out very well for him. They have a solid customer base, even though they only advertise in one specialist publication. Most importantly they're always busy, often doing the kind of specialist work that other places will turn away.

It takes a lot to be an auto technician.

Snap-on

Every year the company will rebuild at least a dozen twelve cylinder Ferrari motors—Patrick is unaware of any other U.S. company doing that. They've got an incredible reputation for what they do, due in no small part to their tight focus on these particular cars. Patrick's engine rebuilder has nearly fifty years experience of working on Ferraris. That's the kind of person you want when your exotic car engine needs some TLC.

Patrick's company will service some modern Ferraris too—his workshop always contains a few mid-engined cars alongside the classic models. Over the years he's witnessed a pattern that ultimately works in his favor. When a new customer first gets involved with Ferraris, they'll usually bring him a modern vehicle. Then, as time goes on, their interest in the older models grows stronger.

So in his experience, most of the modern Ferraris currently coming in for service work will eventually be replaced by one of those older models he loves so dearly.

And love them he does. Patrick owns and drives these cars himself, often taking trips to Italy to compete in classic car events: if that's not love what is?

That love of the cars is the unifying element in his clientele. The owners come from a variety of backgrounds: from successful businesspeople and sports stars to rock and roll guys, these are people in the public eye who've had dramatic success in a relatively short amount of time.

And love them he does. Patrick owns and drives these cars himself . . .

No matter whether they collect their cars or race them—and irrespective of their background—every Ferrari that's brought into Patrick's workshop is loved by its owner.

In this case, loving the cars doesn't mean you want to shout loudly about their location. If you consider the combination of these highly-desirable cars—and the private nature of many of their high-profile owners—a near-camouflaged business exterior suddenly makes complete sense.

Phil Reilly & Co, Inc.

Ross Cummings, Ivan Zaremba, Phil Reilly

5842 Paradise Drive

Corte Madera, California 94925

415-924-9022

Just outside of San Francisco is the town of Corte Madera. Unless you're a resident, this would probably seem much like any other Californian town. If, however you're a car enthusiast, it's got something special going for it—though it's not something that most will get to see.

There is a restoration shop based in this town, known as Phil Reilly & Co. They've been in business longer than I've been alive and have a rock-solid reputation within the automotive industry. It's one of those very uncommon workshops with almost no specialty— that's what makes them unique.

You see, they are primarily known for being experts in the unusual: from pre-war French race cars to Formula One retirees, they do it all. Take a gander at the surrounding pictures and you'll see everything from a Cicistalia coupe to a Sunbeam land-speed- record car, and then you'll notice the various Cosworth engines in different stages of rebuild.

A good example of what they're about is the Bugatti currently under restoration. This is the kind of project that most businesses would be terrified to undertake as the whole restoration has to be accomplished with the guidance of a few decades-old photographs and drawings. Phil Reilly & Co partner, Ivan Zaremba, explains that you have to try and think like Bugatti and build the car like Bugatti would have. This is where they have a distinct advantage over many other similar shops: they have the experience of having worked on similar cars many times before.

You see, they are primarily known for being experts in the unusual . . .

The value of this experience would be hard to overestimate and is often the deciding factor when a well-heeled client is looking for the most suitable restoration shop. After all, this decision does concern their most prized of possessions.

Here's another example: notice in the photographs a Ferrari 250 LM chassis upside-down on a table. This is an original works Le Mans car, which was unfortunately crashed quite recently in an accident back at Le Mans. The car hit the metal barrier at around 90 mph, ultimately receiving damage to three of its four corners.

After getting over the shock, the owner had to get down to business and start shopping for the right restoration shop: they considered businesses the world over. Phil Reilly & Co were able to explain that they'd already restored two other, almost identical, works Le Mans cars. One was restored in the early nineties for well-known clothier Ralph Lauren, and the other was restored thirty-five years ago.

Understandably, this was reassuring news for the car's owner. The Ferrari was duly booked in for the work. On delivery to the shop, it turned out that this was the actual car which Reilly's had already restored thirty-five years ago!

Coincidences like this are not uncommon at Reilly's: the cars will often go through several different lives, yet continually end up back in their workshops. The Birdcage car in the photos was restored by them in 1975, and then once again in 2005. In the meantime it changed hands several times, and apparently lived in at least three different countries.

It would appear that when you get to the type of cars which only exist in extremely small quantities, the number of workshops with relevant experience shrinks dramatically.

Obviously Phil Reilly & Co has earned themselves an enviable reputation, especially within the kind of clientele that can afford such important cars. This reputation is what brings the cars through their doors, but ultimately it's their experience that enables them to send these unique vehicles back out those same doors, finished exactly as they should be.

It's the kind of place that is utterly fascinating to any rare car aficionado, though unfortunately, there are no signs outside to draw you in.

This is not a museum, and it's not open for public perusal because it's a demanding business—they just happen to be working on the kind of cars that we're used to seeing in museums.

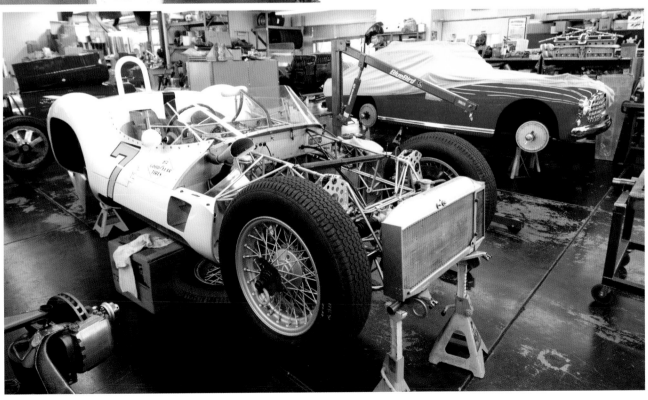

This is not a museum, and it's not open for public perusal . . .

Randy's Foreign Car Clinic

Randy Hutto

5354 Banks Street, Suite A

San Diego, California 92110

619-299-2994

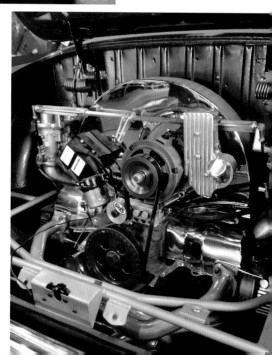

There was a time, not too long ago, when San Diego County seemed to be overflowing with repair shops for vintage air-cooled Volkswagens. This area has always been in love with the air-cooled generation of these cars, perhaps more so than any other part of California.

The weather here had been so kind on these cars, they barely corroded. Word got out and it wasn't long before people from all around the world would fly into San Diego to find a nice old car to take back home. Consequently most of the classic VWs have long since scattered to the four winds.

As the cars leave, there are fewer local customers for the repair shops. Over the years many had to close their doors, or specialize in something new. Not Randy's Foreign Car Clinic.

Randy's has been around since 1980, all the while specializing in Volkswagens. Now their core business is VWs built pre-1991, including the Vans, Bugs, Ghias, and Buses. They will also take in newer models when asked to do so by a loyal customer—it's not unusual to have an '03 Beetle being serviced next to an original '53 Bug.

The owner, Randy Hutto, explains that while a big part of the business is daily repairs of cars that people are still driving, there's also a lot in the way of restoration work. Randy is seeing a resurgence of locals who are pulling their old cars out of their yards and bringing them in, either due to high gas prices or just nostalgia. He also has plenty of customers who handed their old Bugs down to their children who now use them regularly and so still have them serviced at Randy's.

Others, who let the cars sit unused for years, now want them totally restored. While Randy's does all the mechanical restoration in-house, they send out the body and paintwork to a local specialist—in Mexico. It might seem odd to say that this "local" specialist is in Mexico, but if you look at San Diego's location on a map, you'll see it makes sense.

The advantage to using a body and paint specialist in Mexico is that it makes Randy's one of the only places where you can have your old car re-sprayed using the original factory paints. These paints have been outlawed in the U.S. This is advantageous because the modern replacement paints are much more prone to blistering and popping anywhere from a few months to a year after being painted.

Randy's also has a great local upholstery firm who can match all of the original colors used in these great old cars. Sending out the body, paint, and upholstery means that they can continue to concentrate on doing all of the mechanical and electrical work in-house, while keeping their business the right size.

Randy has seen other shops get too big in the good times, and then need to downsize in the hard times—sometimes this yo-yo growing and downsizing has killed the company completely. Surviving with such a specific focus for twenty-eight years says a lot about this business.

The only potential problem for Randy's Foreign Car Clinic at this point would be caused by all of the remaining air-cooled VWs leaving southern California. Thankfully that's unlikely to happen, as the locals now value what's left. It's now not uncommon to see VW ads where the seller says, "No out of area buyers please!"

. . . there's also a lot in the way of restoration work.

Salerno Motorsports

Ben and Janet Salerno

4322 Anthony Court, #8

Rocklin, California 95677

916-652-0496

People get into the automotive world for a variety of reasons, though some will forget along the way what it was that initially drew them in. Not Ben Salerno—he couldn't have ended up anywhere else.

Ben was the youngest of four boys and was fascinated by all things mechanical going as far back as his family can remember. Once, when Ben was just a kid, his father was throwing away a lawnmower and Ben asked for the engine. He somehow managed to attach that tiny motor to his bicycle, making some kind of Mad Max-looking mini bike. He then proceeded to ride this creation around the neighborhood until he was issued a ticket. Apparently the stern-faced cop wasn't too impressed with the lad's mechanical ingenuity and charged him with "riding a motorized vehicle without a permit."

Thankfully, it didn't dampen his enthusiasm. He was soon rebuilding entire car engines in the family driveway: this before he was old enough to drive. He took every auto shop class offered, and by the time he was sixteen he already had his smog license!

He somehow managed to attach
that tiny motor to his bicycle . . .

To say that Ben liked vehicles would
be a huge understatement. When
he was nineteen he bought himself
a 1970 Porsche 911S—his wife still
says that this car is his first true
love. You'll notice the phrase "is his
first true love" is in the present
tense. That's because Ben has
never been able to bring himself
to sell the car.

Before that car he toyed around
with some other cool stuff, a Volvo
P1800, a Triumph Stag, a Trans Am
that lasted about a month before
he decided it just wasn't for him,
and then another 1800 Volvo. At
one point his mechanical mind got
the better of him and he even
turbocharged one of those Volvos,
but that's another story.

"I love it, I love the technology. I love the challenge of repairing it . . .

It was the Porsche that would prove to be the most pivotal vehicle, as it's what ultimately led him to where he is now. His first taste of a 911 was a car that his old boss let him drive once after Ben had worked on it. That was it—he was totally addicted. Buying his own 911 confirmed to him how great they really were, and now Ben and his wife, Janet, are immersed in the world of Porsche. They run a shop called Salerno Motorsports which specializes in Ferrari, Porsche, BMW, and Mercedes: but it's the Ferraris and Porsches that really stir Ben's passion.

At Salerno, they will undertake everything from service to full restoration of their customer's cars. Over the years, Ben has restored a Ferrari 250 PF and regularly services a 275 Spider, but it's the mid-engined stuff that really does it for him—particularly the 430. What's interesting is that the modern Ferraris are very intimidating to most mechanics because of their complex electronics. Not to Ben—in fact he's quite the opposite,

"I love it, I love the technology. I love the challenge of repairing it, I love the diagnostics of it, I love the new stuff!" He continues, "I've been exposed to it all, and there's no question that my passion is the newest, most modern. The next model is my favorite!"

So as a customer, this makes Salerno Motorsports a pretty safe bet to look after your high-dollar, high-tech supercar. Ben Salerno will sometimes even have a Ferrari of his own: as you can imagine, with his love for the most modern of modern cars, they change pretty often.

Amidst all of those other cars there's always that old '70 911S which started it all. He's tweaked that car significantly over the years. Now it produces around 450 horsepower while weighing in at a mere 2500 pounds, but that's to be expected really.

At least Ben now has the relevant vehicle permit . . .

Santo's Italian Car Service

Santo Rimicci

8816 Amigo Avenue.

Northridge, California 91324

818-701-1614

Part of the appeal of an Italian car is a wider appreciation of the wonderful Italian culture, of the passion which is an integral part of the Italian spirit. Practically this means that most people don't like their Italian cars, they love 'em.

When you love your car, it's a little stressful trying to gauge if you can trust somebody enough to fix it: enter Santo's Italian Car Service. The owner, Santo Rimicci, is a Sicilian, long ago transplanted to California. He learned in his youth how to fix cars as an apprentice back in Italy. By '81 he had moved his family stateside and set up his own shop in Northridge, just outside of Los Angeles.

Santo's specializes in Alfa Romeos—as that make was the owner's first mechanical love—though Santo's will repair any and all Italian cars. The variety they handle makes a trip to their premises exciting for any lover of classic Italian metal: from GTVs to rarities like a Montreal, the shop's usually got something in that'll quicken the pulse.

Unlike some other shops, mechanical repairs are what Santo's is all about: they don't get involved with bodywork or paint at all. Sticking to the mechanical stuff means that Santo and his son, Anthony, have developed very deep knowledge on the subject, enough to build and run race cars. Anthony successfully campaigns a '65 GTA in vintage racing, regularly beating glamorous Porsche 911s and 904s in his almost innocent-looking little Alfa.

Practically this means that most people don't like their Italian cars, they love 'em.

If the Alfa looks innocent, it's a bit of a trick. His '65 is actually a former works race car, which makes it both a serious track tool and a rare bird to boot. Being so involved in the scene, if anyone can turn up a car like that, it's these Italian gentlemen.

Over the years, Anthony's track success has gradually brought more business into their shop. If a young guy blows your Italian car into the weeds—in a car that's tuned and maintained in his own Italian car workshop—

you're going to be curious what that same workshop can do for your car. With the growth of that business they now maintain, tune up, and improve around twenty other vintage Italian race cars. Thus, the Santo's workshop logo is a common sight at California's vintage racing events.

So what do the guys who keep everybody else's Italian cars in tip-top shape use to get to work and back every day? Would it be surprising to hear they even

commute in classic Alfa Romeos? For the work journey, the cars of choice are 1970s era GTVs. As Anthony says, "Over here in California you can still drive them year round. They're my favorite car ever. You can drive them every day, you can race them, you can take them to car shows. It's a really good all-around car."

When you love your Alfa Romeos the way they do, to commute in any other car would almost be like cheating, and cheating on an Italian is a big no no.

Scott Motors

Gary Prothero

2257 South Federal Avenue.

West Los Angeles, California 90064

310-231-4460

Rolls-Royces are not what you would call common cars: you don't see numerous models grounded in traffic on your daily commute. Actually most of us are unlikely to see even one solitary Rolls-Royce on our commute. You could go as far as saying they're an unusual sight.

Unless you live in Beverly Hills.

The Beverly Hills, Malibu, Santa Monica, and West Los Angeles neighborhoods all border each other, and are all pretty affluent areas. Disposable income is the key element here. If you live in a quaint midwestern town—where a 2,000 square foot house for $150,000 is something to aspire to—then a new $350,000 Rolls would most likely look like an unfathomable extravagance. However, if you're living in an area where an 11,000 square foot house can sell for $25,000,000 without raising too many eyebrows, then a Rolls-Royce is potentially more of an impulse buy.

Considering all of the above, if you were going to find a Rolls-Royce specialist anywhere, it's most likely going to be here. The best-known independent Rolls-Royce and Bentley specialty shop in the west L.A. area is Scott Motors, owned by a British expat named Gary Prothero.

Gary has been working on Rollers almost his whole life. When he first came to America in 1968 he worked for a Rolls-Royce dealer in Boston, where he stayed until '75. Finally the idea of weather that was actually different from his native England lured him to southern California.

After a stint as a shop foreman for a Beverly Hills dealership, he decided to go solo. After a few twists and turns he ended up here, at the helm of his own specialty workshop. Scott Motors employs three mechanics, and Gary's son runs the parts operation. They only work on Rolls-Royce and Bentley, and stick to the mechanical work on these fine cars.

They've labored on some very old models over the years . . .

They've labored on some very old models over the years, but Gary's happiest working on cars from the fifties through to newer models which are just out of warranty. The only models of Rolls-Royce that he avoids are the GTs and the Phantoms, explaining that they are so far removed from what he's accustomed to that they wouldn't be able to give them the type of service that his company is known for.

Occasionally a customer will come in asking if Scott Motors can perform a full restoration on their old car. The guys will happily do this, but only by working in conjunction with one of the local area's best body shops.

When asked what the typical customer is like for a Rolls-Royce specialist in this world-famous region of California, Gary can't find any obvious commonality: they range from showbiz people through the music industry into real estate and just regular residents of the area.

Gary has been working on Rollers almost his whole life.

Looking in as an outsider, maybe the typical Rolls-Royce-driving customer in the home of America's most expensive zip codes is more easily defined as anybody who can comfortably afford to buy a nice house in Beverly Hills!

Stewart's European Auto Specialists

Stewart L. Rosen

1876 Stockton Boulevard

Sacramento, California 95816

916-731-7023

In Sacramento back in the sixties, there was a Maserati dealership based in a highly-visible location on the edge of a bustling intersection. The dealership was called John's Automotive and among its many employees was a young man named Stewart Rosen.

After a few years working in the Maserati dealership, Stewart felt he was ready to go solo. The elderly owner of John's Automotive was happy to help him find his feet, even though Stewart was opening up his business next door. A little later on, the former Maserati dealership's building became available (the original owner was retiring) so Stewart took over the building he'd once worked in.

Now Stewart's European Auto Specialists operates from a wonderful spot in Sacramento, one that even the oldest of locals still associates with European cars. Having learned the ropes on Maseratis, the Italian brand is one of several which Stewart will repair. He also concentrates on Rolls-Royce, Bentley, and Ferrari, but the biggest part of Stewart's business by far comes from Jaguar and Land Rover owners.

Stewart is happiest for his staff to work on the newest of these vehicles. Practically, that translates to late model cars over three years old, due to the familiar issue of manufacturer's warranty requirements.

While these vehicles form the core of their business, it's certainly not all they do. Stewart Rosen has been in the industry so long that many locals feel he's the person to take their classic car to, especially for major work. This means it's not uncommon for their workshops to contain everything from Range Rovers to E-types, and Discoverys to Jaguar XK120s.

While restorations aren't necessarily the kind of work that Stewart looks for, he can never say no to them either, mainly because he's so passionate about these beautiful old cars. Where restorations are concerned, Stewart's sticks to the mechanical side. Bodywork is not their specialty so it's always trusted to local specialist Brian Moore, who is covered in another chapter.

Now Stewart's European Auto Specialists operates from a wonderful spot in Sacramento . . .

While he loves the oldies, he's recently been favoring the modern breed of sports cars for his own use. One of his most recent drivers was a Maserati Cambia Corsa. He'd been using it regularly for some time, and felt he'd bought a car comparable to a Ferrari 360 for considerably less money. The problem came when the Maserati went in for some bodywork. The repairs took some time, and when Stewart drove a Ferrari 360 to the body shop to pick up his Maserati: well, the direct comparison wasn't favorable. On getting back behind the wheel of the Maserati he remembers, "I thought I was driving a Volkswagen bus."

Now Stewart owns a 360 himself, and Ferraris are one of his passions at work too. He estimates that in 2008, he spent around $60,000 on keeping his tools and diagnostic software up to date so that the shop could offer its customers a full Ferrari repair service.

This need to keep current with the diagnostic systems for modern cars is ultimately what causes certain shops to concentrate on just one or two brands of vehicle. Any more is too much of a financial commitment for most independents.

While many privately-owned workshops are looking at ways to reduce their expenses, Stewart's is looking at specializing in a couple more brands. Jaguar and Land Rover vehicles keep them busy right now, but Stewart noticed that usage of Land Rovers and Range Rovers dropped off with the 2008 spike in fuel prices. With a finite amount of fossil fuels left, it's likely that high gas prices will become as common in the U.S. as they are on other continents.

Unless Land Rover starts importing a diesel-powered vehicle into America, he feels that their Land Rover business might gradually drop off. These are the kind of potential problems that any intelligent business owner has to see coming. It's also indicative of the kind of thinking that has taken Stewart from being a young employee to the successful owner of a high-end European car workshop.

SVS Automotive Corporation

Robert Marcello

2009 Fulton Avenue.

Sacramento, California 95825

916-971-1382

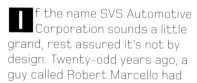

If the name SVS Automotive Corporation sounds a little grand, rest assured it's not by design. Twenty-odd years ago, a guy called Robert Marcello had decided it was time to stop being an employee in the automotive business. He was ready to go it alone. He had previously started concentrating on Volvos, partially because few other people wanted to, and also because he respected the overbuilt way they engineered their cars.

So he set up a new business called Sacramento's Volvo Service. As he wasn't a franchised dealership, he was soon politely asked to change this name. The rename, which still stands, incorporates a recognizable element of the original: SVS Automotive.

In those early days he had two other guys working with him, and their collective aim was simply to earn enough to get by. Within a short amount of time they had developed a six-week waiting list for service work, and this trend continued for nearly a year. They realized that they had to grow, grow again, and grow some more. Now they're one of the biggest nonfranchised shops in the area, with twelve full-time employees. And, interestingly, all three original guys are still happily coexisting within the workplace.

Customers often couldn't believe how much better their car performed . . .

Robert tracks what's happening with his business very effectively and can quote payroll figures and monthly income off the top of his head. He also knows that his regular customer base currently stands at 3,600 people and that it's the people that matter. He is very fond of saying, "We're here to service the people, not the cars."

Obviously a big part of keeping those people happy is in the way they service those cars. In the early days, when Robert was wielding the wrenches, he would always spend more time on the customers' cars than the bill showed. What he was doing with the extra time was the same for every customer: he'd be checking the things that never got checked. He'd drive the car up and down the street making sure the steering wheel was centered perfectly, he'd make sure the wipers parked at the right angle on the windshield, and he'd make sure that the linkages were adjusted correctly.

Now they're one of the biggest nonfranchised shops in the area . . .

Customers often couldn't believe how much better their car performed because "Now it had full throttle!"

207

SVS has outgrown their original service bay a few times, and each time they do, they take on another adjoining building. Now they not only have a very impressive modern service facility, they also have an in-house exhaust shop where they can make custom systems. They also have their own research and development building and an engine rebuild shop where they'll even do performance upgrades.

If it seems odd having an engine shop which takes pride in creating more horsepower when you're primarily working on sensible cars like Volvos, Robert will explain that it's not. They actually go together better than you'd expect. He finds that if a customer's car needs some repair work to the cylinder head, most people will gladly pay a little more to have it ported, polished, and balanced. The reason is simple: the typical owner wants to have the work done only once and anything that will make it run better and longer is a completely justifiable expense for them.

He's also noticed that Volvo owners are typically purists: they love their Volvos because they're not like other cars. In his local area he's noticed that sales have been gradually dropping since Ford started "crossbreeding" them. You'd think that reduced sales of new cars would be worrying for a privately-owned Volvo specialist, but his customers have given him no cause for concern. They just plan to keep their existing cars longer, and he's more than happy to be a part of that.

Swedish American Imports

Chuck Porter

1635 Ohms Way, Suite E

Costa Mesa, California 92627

949-646-7731

Even in California, some European cars outnumber others. With late model cars this can be observed on the streets, with the old car scene you'll easily notice which cars are the most popular at the classic car gatherings and, finally, you can see what's popular by the number of workshops that exist to look after each specific car.

Though specialists in the various cars from Sweden are few and far between, one very reputable and long-term established specialist can be found in Costa Mesa.

Based in the back streets of this town is Swedish American Imports, operated by Chuck Porter. Chuck's seen many changes over the years in the California car scene. So many of the old classic cars he used to work on were gradually sold to visiting Europeans who'd come to California solely to find a rust-free car. Slowly the quantity of classic Swedish cars started to dry up.

Chuck still works on the same cars he's always worked on: Saabs, both new and old, Volvos, both modern and classic, and the legendary Rolls-Royce too. With the Rollers, Chuck sticks to the early nineties cars and older, as there's just too much electronic equipment on the more recent stuff.

Currently he's in the middle of a couple of long-term vintage Rolls-Royce projects, a 1928 four-cylinder convertible and a 1934 six-cylinder convertible. They're not restorations as such, more like renovations. He's already cleaned, sandblasted, and repainted the frame on the '34, as well as polished all of the unpainted metal parts. The plan is for that car to be driven, not just shown, so usability is prioritized over prettiness.

Chuck used to do considerably more in the way of restoration. Until very recently, he owned a second business called Sir Charles Limited that was solely a body and paint shop. But Chuck's been doing this for a long time and is starting to wind things down a little. He closed down his Sir Charles business, feeling that he's got plenty to keep him busy with Swedish American, which focuses on service work.

Now the customers get tired of the car long before it's worn out!

He still gets suckered into a restoration here and there—like the two vintage Rollers he has in—but the bread and butter work now is in looking after the modern Swedish stuff. Impressively the modern Saabs and Volvos need very little to keep them at their best. He explains that it's much more common now to have to replace brakes on a car and leave the engine almost completely alone. The older generations of Volvos (he still has five or six regulars) needed a valve job occasionally, but those days are gone. Now the customers get tired of the car long before it's worn out!

So maybe the Swedish cars aren't that scarce at all: there's a strong possibility that one of the reasons for finding so few Swedish car repair shops is that the cars just never need fixing . . .

Chuck sticks to the early nineties cars and older.

Swiss Motors

Robert Husser

3929 Sepulveda Boulevard

Culver City, California 90230

310-398-5111

husser@swissmotors.com

In Culver City there is a German car workshop owned by two Swiss transplants, Robert Husser and Marcel Bont. Naturally it's known as Swiss Motors. Robert and Marcel have been in business in this location for around twenty years, and have settled on Mercedes-Benz, BMW, Porsche and VW/Audi as their core business.

Until around ten years ago they also worked on Ferraris but, due to regular hassles getting the parts, they've simplified their lives by stopping work on that particular brand. Now they're left with all of the big German names which are as popular in the shop owners' native country of Switzerland as they are in the cars' own German homeland.

Many of you already know that Switzerland not only borders Germany, but Italy and France as well. Most of its citizens are fluent in German, French, and Italian, so there's a strong affinity for all things from these bordering countries.

Swiss Motors will go quite far back with the vehicles from these manufacturers. For example, they'll work on Porsches just out of warranty and also regularly work on cars as old as the original Porsche—the gorgeous and iconic 356. With Mercedes they'll go back as far as the 230SLs, and with VW, they'll work on anything that's water-cooled.

Like many businesses that concentrate on the mechanical work, they will only undertake restorations by working in conjunction with good local body and upholstery shops, but they find that restorations aren't that common anyway. Their local customer base provides way more in the way of refurbishment work: as Robert explains, "It actually happens more often than restorations with us. Most people over here, they're enjoying still driving them, not just parking them. If you want to drive it, you don't want to restore it the whole way."

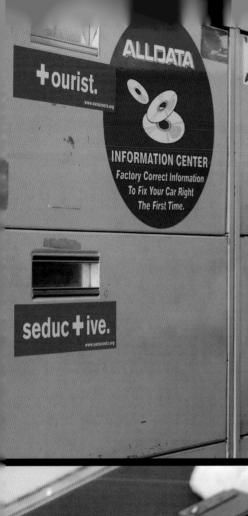

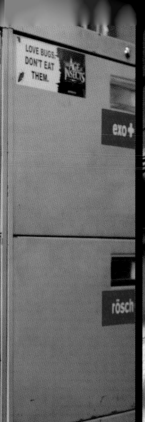

Swiss Motors

Being from a country that's so different in so many ways, he's also very aware of how much longer these old models can last in California's idyllic climate. You never have to take a torch to a bolt in the sunny state, he explains, unlike northern Europe where corrosion is like a fast-acting form of vehicular cancer.

Like so many other European workshops, their daily stuff isn't necessarily the most interesting stuff that they undertake. It's not requested very often but Swiss Motors is more than capable of doing some very trick work—take Robert's own vehicle as an example.

In '93 he bought an '81 Volkswagen Vanagon, powered by the stock (factory-detuned) 2.0 liter engine. By '94 he felt it was too weak so he fitted a Porsche 3.2 liter engine and a T50 transmission. When asked what the combination is like, he answers in a way that would surprise the average American: "It's been very reliable."

It makes about 230 horsepower, so it's safe to assume that it goes quite well too. Apparently Robert has kept the Vanagon as a real sleeper, which must make it a whole lot of fun to drive in car-crazy California.

. . . and with VW, they'll work on anything that's water-cooled.

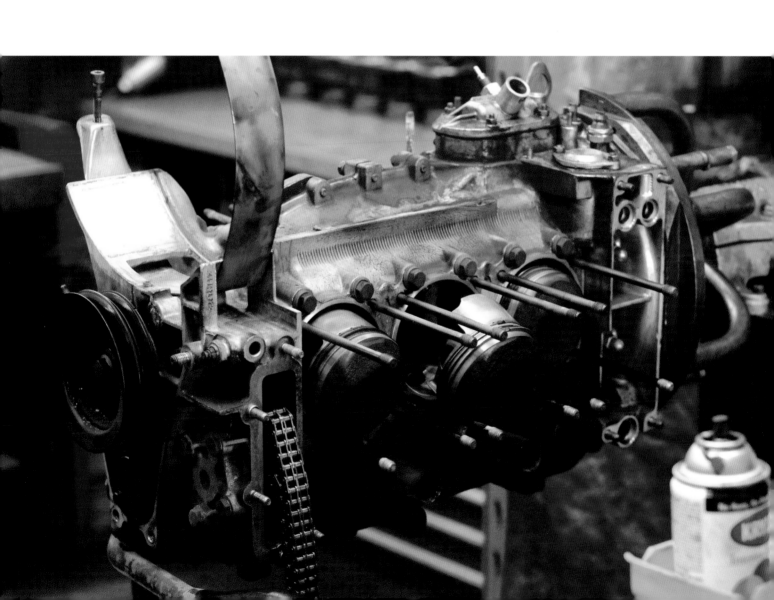

Symbolic Motor Car Company

Bruce Marquand

11455 Sorrento Valley Road

San Diego, California 92121

858-350-1393

bruce@symbolicmotors.com

For many people, the Symbolic Motor Car Company needs no introduction. Their showroom in La Jolla is well known, drawing car enthusiasts and collectors from across the country. The showroom is a fascinating place to look around because of the variety of cars it contains.

But Symbolic has another building, one that's potentially more interesting for the purposes of this book. The location of their other premises isn't widely known, because it doesn't need to be. This isn't another showroom for the public to peruse: it's their restoration center and is one of the most comprehensive restoration shops on the entire west coast. These premises are so vast, it's quite possibly one of the biggest restoration premises in existence. What's most surprising is that it's relatively new.

Back in 2004, Symbolic decided to adopt this 30,000 square-foot building for their new restoration shop which (at the time) employed five restoration guys. Shop manager, Bruce Marquand, still remembers thinking, "How are we gonna fill this thing?"

Now, just four years later, they have twenty-five restoration department employees and the huge building is bursting at the seams—so much so that they've started using shipping containers for additional external storage.

So what goes on in this cavernous space? In a word, everything. There are storage rooms for the cars the company has recently purchased as well as those just out of the restoration shop awaiting delivery. There's an in-house parts department, a metal shop, a body shop, a paint shop, a machine shop, a motor assembly room, and a huge bay that serves as a combination maintenance and service area. There's even an in-house photo studio where they shoot the cars for their own advertisements!

He's always kept pace with the changes in automotive technology . . .

If Symbolic doesn't impress you, it's likely that nothing in the car world can. Inside their machine shop and engine room they have the ability to gas flow cylinder heads and can build everything from an original MGC works motor to a fully-machined Ferrari 275 engine.

Though their restoration business may not have been here very long, the company more than makes up for it with the experience of their employees. For some time now, they've been poaching specialists and enlarging their in-house skill set. Often they will employ senior guys—experts who could almost certainly earn more with a new car manufacturer—but their passion for these exquisite cars keeps them here.

One such valued employee, Sydney Carr, is Jim Clarke's race car spanner man from Jim's 1960s glory days. Sidney has gone from working on Jim's Formula One and Formula Two cars to working on Formula 3000s now. He's always kept pace with the changes in automotive technology and is still an expert, though now it's with the most complex of modern engine management systems.

Completed cars roll out of Symbolic's restoration shop and sometimes head straight off to win trophies at shows like Pebble Beach. It's no surprise then that the company's reputation has already resulted in customers shipping cars from the other side of the country: several Florida cars were being restored at the time of our photo shoot. Bruce Marquand explains that most of their business still comes from Southern California, as many of their customers have "at least one house in California . . ."

And that is, of course, the reality of vintage racecar and Italian supercar ownership—it usually goes with a lavish lifestyle. If that sounds like you, then the Symbolic Motor Car Company needs to be at the top (or at least near the top) of your "recommended" list.

For the rest of us, we'll just enjoy the photographs and dream.

There's even an in-house photo studio where they shoot the cars . . .

Ted Blake's Porsche and VW

2701 21st Street

Sacramento, California 95818

916-455-5010

Ted Blake is a seventy–one-year-old Porsche 356 expert, though some would say that statement doesn't carry enough weight. They would claim that he is, in fact, "the" Porsche expert.

He's been working on old Porches and Volkswagens forever: he ran a VW and Porsche repair shop in another downtown location for twenty-odd years and has been at his current location for another twenty-one. These days most of his business is full ground-up restorations of vintage Porsche 356 models.

It wasn't always this way—he used to do a lot of work on air-cooled VWs too. There's an urban legend in the area based around the town's two franchised Volkswagen dealerships. The story goes that VW of America asked local customers which of the town's two VW dealerships they preferred, and Ted Blake won by a write-in vote. Interesting, considering he wasn't one of the two!

Anyway, it goes a long way in explaining the kind of reputation that Ted has. Perhaps a better illustration of the kind of respect Ted has earned is in the fact that he has ten years worth of work ahead of him, already booked. As unbelievable as that sounds, it's the reality here at Ted Blake's. The car in the process of being stripped down in the accompanying images was on the waiting list for nine years.

Thankfully Ted isn't working alone: he currently has two "trainees," both retired from their original careers and working with Ted because they share the passion for these incredible little cars. The disadvantage to the more "mature" labor that Ted employs is that they've been know to take time off to play golf now and again . . .

When the cars reach the top of Ted's unbelievable waiting list and are finally allowed into his hallowed workshop, the first stage is figuring out what's previously happened to them. All of these cars are over forty years old, and multiple welded patches are a typical issue. There's no doubt that the biggest issue for a Porsche 356 is rust.

The cars are fully dismantled—
right down to the chassis—then
sent out for media blasting. When
they come back, any rusted or
dented areas are clearly visible.
At this point any body panels
with problems are replaced—
apparently there are still some
excellent quality replacement
panels available. Ted cuts the
panels out along the same seams
where the factory welded them in,
meaning that when they're finished
they'll look identical to how they
left the factory.

The next stage is to send the
shell off to the paint shop. This is
where most customers will opt to
correct the multiple color changes
that have previously taken place
and return the car to its original
factory-applied paint color.

Upon return, the car is mounted
into a rotisserie, allowing the
guys to flip the car upside down.
They'll then spray the underside of
the car with an underseal, being
careful to also inject it into any
hollow body sections to ensure
maximum rust resistance.

As the car goes back together,
every single nut and bolt is either
restored or replaced. At this point
there are a few modifications
that Ted will recommend, things
like a dual master cylinder for the
brakes for safety reasons. Some
customers will make several other
"improvements," like running a later
motor from a 912, or upgrading
to a 12 volt electrical system.
The majority of his customers,
however, are purists who prefer
to avoid unnecessary changes.

He's been working on old Porsches and Volkswagens forever...

The final part of one of his restorations is the engine, as Ted is reluctant to have a "built" engine sitting around unused. He'll always bench run the engine and make final adjustments before fitting it to the completed car. Once this is all done, it allows the next customer on his ten-year waiting list to finally bring their car into this legendary Porsche workshop.

Before moving on, it's worthy of mention that the only unrestored 356 parked outside every day is Ted's own daily driver. Isn't there some old saying about cobblers and their shoes?

Thunder Ranch

Tom McBurnie

1410 Pioneer Way

El Cajon, California 92020

619-444-1006

tmcburnie@thunderranch.com

Almost every workshop in this book is in the business of restoring or maintaining cars originally made in Europe. A shop just outside San Diego called Thunder Ranch is, however, coming at the European car scene from a slightly different direction.

Company owner and main designer, Thomas McBurnie, is in the business of creating replicas of early Porsches. These cars may lack originality in the eyes of a diehard Porsche purist, but they're vastly superior in terms of usability, something greatly appreciated by his many customers.

Thunder Ranch vehicles are brand new cars. Built in a way that's true to early Porsche designs, they benefit from modern technological improvements, as long as those improvements are in accord with the original Porsche design ethic. Specifically, this means that if an original car would have been fitted with a horizontally-opposed, air-cooled engine, so are these new cars—they're just powered by a better one.

Thunder Ranch offers an impressive selection of models, including three versions of the 550 Spyder, a car immortalized by actor James Dean. The first is a model almost identical to the original car, and the second is an "A version" featuring fender flares which fit a one-and-a-half inch wider wheel. The third version is powered by a modern six cylinder Porsche 911 motor.

Thunder also makes two versions of Porsche 356 Speedster (their wide-bodied variant is known as the Phantom), and two versions of the 718RSK. They even have two more cars currently under development: a 336-type vehicle, based on the first Porsche ever built, and a 904-inspired car, after Porsche's first-ever fiberglass vehicle.

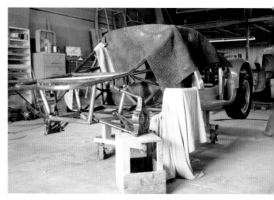

By the time Ferdinand Porsche started building the cars that bore his name, he'd already designed the Volkswagen Beetle, and a lot of Beetle parts were interchangeable with his early Porsche models. Even looking closely at the current Porsche 911, the lineage is apparent.

At Thunder Ranch, in keeping with the cars' European roots, a great deal of each vehicle is constructed with new Volkswagen Beetle parts. As something like 56 million VW Bugs were manufactured over the years, the parts availability for them is absolutely excellent. While all of the moving components on Thunder Ranch vehicles are brand new, some other essential parts are no longer in production, parts like transaxles. This is where Tom's people will source original Bugs and completely rebuild the relevant original parts.

. . . they benefit from modern technological improvements . . .

If you take a look at the specs of one of his cars (let's pick the Speedster) the benefits of the modern upgrades become obvious. The original car weighed in at around 1780 lb, but his fiberglass-bodied cars weigh in at 1551 lb. The original car had a 70 hp motor—his cars can be powered by engines producing up to 170 hp. The original had drum brakes all round with a swing axle rear—his have disk brakes up front, and a full IRS back-end. One of Tom's cars will, quite simply, leave an original for dead on the street.

Yes, but there's more to it than that. The originals are worth considerably more, and that makes them more nerve wracking to drive. Tom McBurnie's cars are fast, efficient, immune from rust, and just as good looking as the originals. They're also safer under hard driving and comparatively stress free, a combination that's proving to be more than enough for a great many car fans.

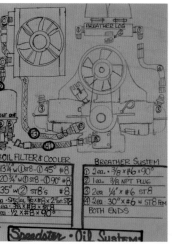

This is where Tom's people will source original Bugs and completely rebuild the relevant original parts.

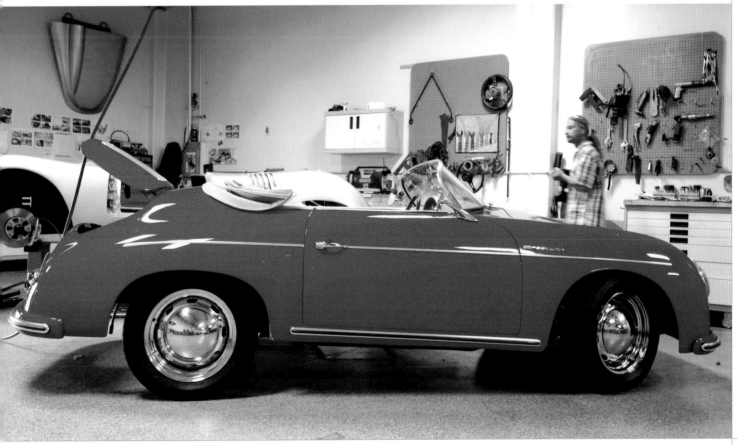

Tony Handler, Inc.

2028 Cotner Avenue

Los Angeles, California 90025

(310) 473-7773

The variety of specialist car shops in California is staggering, but even in such a diverse area, the best way to describe this particular auto business is "unlikely."

Take a look at the ingredients: in the middle of well-to-do West Los Angeles is a cramped, dirty workshop that dismantles old English cars down to the last piece. They then store the oily parts on shelves out in clear view until customers who can't find that component anywhere else in the world purchase them one piece at a time.

This business is Tony Handler, Inc. and it's famous in Rolls-Royce and Bentley circles. As head honcho, Tony Handler, says: "We're like aspirin for Rolls-Royce parts: if you own one of these cars, you know us!" Tony is a very charismatic Rolls-Royce aficionado who has been in this business for thirty-eight years and counting.

All his business does is dismantle post-war Rolls-Royce and Bentley cars for their parts. They do no repair work, no service, and no restoration. In fact what they will do on a customer's car is best summed up by Tony himself: "I love my customers dearly, but all I'll do is check their oil!"

This is a parts business, plain
and simple. The cars in the
accompanying images are mostly
vehicles that are being dismantled,
though some are Tony's personal
vehicles. Once the cars are
stripped down, the parts can end
up literally anywhere—there's
barely a country in the world Tony
hasn't sold to. He laughs when he
explains how much he sells back to
England, the cars' original home.

To non-Rolls owners it may
be shocking to learn how new
the donor cars can be: it's not
uncommon for him to strip down a
vehicle that's less than ten years
old. Parts availability is surprisingly
poor, even on the newer models.
Service shops worldwide are often
desperate for the pieces needed
to return their customers'
vehicles to the road.

. . . the best way
to describe this
particular auto
business is "unlikely."

Tony Handler, Inc.

With many makes, buying from a dismantler is often one of many options—it's usually the cheap route when compared to buying new from various sources. In the case of these cars, it can be the only option for procuring the required parts.

With thirty-eight years worth of inventory, everybody has to deal with Tony Handlers. He even sells parts to franchised dealerships. "We are a sort of necessary evil, even for the authorized dealers who don't want to admit it. They buy a lot from us!"

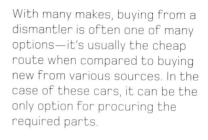

What remains unlikely is the prospect of him staying in West L.A. indefinitely, with his open-air shelves stacked sky high with parts. He's already had to cover the top of his shelving units to appease complaints from local residents and office workers who'd been looking down on something not to their sophisticated tastes. Slightly ironic, considering that many of these complainers would love to actually own a Rolls-Royce.

Maybe then they'd appreciate Tony Handler.

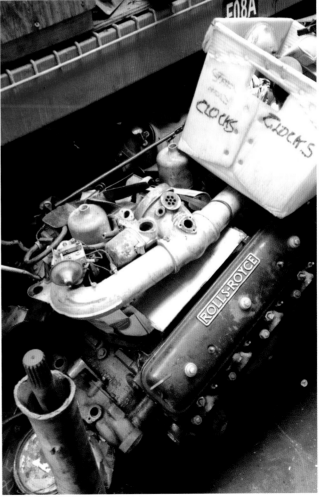

He laughs when he explains how much he sells back to England . . .

Viking Motorsports, Inc.

Harry R. Appleby

3019 Enterprise Street

Costa Mesa, California 92626

714-979-1020

vikingmotorsports@sbcglobal.net

Costa Mesa is known for its shopping mall, of all things. Apparently its South Coast Plaza is one of the highest-volume regional shopping centers in the U.S. If octane stirs your blood more than a pair of new shoes, then Costa Mesa is more interesting for its abundance of specialty car workshops.

One standout business in the area is Viking Motorsports, owned by an expatriate Brit named Harry Appleby. Harry has been involved with British sports cars since the sixties back in Britain, where he originally started working on Lotuses.

He's been at his current location for eight years, where he's earned a loyal following for his skilled work on Lotuses. He also specializes in Jensen-Healeys (which were fitted with Lotus motors), plus Jaguars, MGs, Triumphs, Rovers, Bentleys, and Rolls-Royces: basically if it's British and runs on gas, he knows how to make it purr.

Harry has observed a divide in what people want from their British sports cars, and it's most commonly broken down by the vehicle's age. If you go back to the early cars—like the Lotus Elan—customers are mostly purists, valuing originality above all. When you get to the later cars, most of the customers are after better performance, which Viking is more than capable of supplying.

... customers are mostly purists, valuing originality above all.

On the four cylinder cars—like the Esprits—Viking can do chip upgrades which have the potential to raise the power output to a whopping 350 horsepower. In a lightweight car like a Lotus, that's an intimidating figure.

With the eight cylinder cars, the standard output is 350 horsepower, and 400 horsepower can be achieved relatively easily, even with the standard pistons. For serious results, Harry recommends rebuilding the turbo, blueprinting the motor, fitting forged pistons, using ARP head studs and the race ECU: with those mods the engine can realize its true 450 horsepower potential. Harry explains that you can build a motor capable of even more than that, but it just becomes trouble waiting to happen.

Results can be gained with early Elans too—like Harry's own '67—but most people simply aren't after that. Interestingly, Harry brought his Elan over from England with him, when he first came to the US in '82. This particular Lotus wasn't actually built by Lotus—it was built by Harry, using original parts that he'd collected over the years. He estimates that his car was built by parts from five other cars!

While Viking specializes in Lotus cars, they're not a franchised dealer for the new models (though he does have a good relationship with the company). It's not surprising that many of his loyal customers still bring their new cars into his very highly-regarded workshop anyway.

Aside from his Lotus, Harry also owns a supercharged XJR Jaguar and a series three Vanden Plas with a quarter million miles on the clock.

Harry Appleby is clearly in this business for the love of the cars, which means that—just like the rest of us—octane is in his blood.

Harry has been involved with British sports cars since the sixties.

239

Index